Welcome to the Board!

An Orientation for the New Health Care Trustee

Health Research and Educational Trust of New Jersey

JOSSEY-BASS
A Wiley Imprint
www.josseybass.com

Health Forum, Inc.
An American Hospital Association Company
CHICAGO press

Published by Jossey-Bass
A Wiley Imprint
989 Market Street, San Francisco, CA 94103-1741   www.josseybass.com

ΛHΛ is a service mark of the American Hospital Association used under license by AHA Press

This publication is designed to provide accurate and authoritative information in regard to the subject matter covered. It is sold with the understanding that neither the authors nor the publisher is engaged in rendering legal, accounting, or other professional services. If legal advice or other expert assistance is required, the services of a competent professional person should be sought.

The views expressed in this book are strictly those of the authors and do not represent official positions of the American Hospital Association.

Jossey-Bass books and products are available through most bookstores. To contact Jossey-Bass directly call our Customer Care Department within the U.S. at 800-956-7739, outside the U.S. at 317-572-3986 or fax 317-572-4002.

Jossey-Bass also publishes its books in a variety of electronic formats. Some content that appears in print may not be available in electronic books.

Cover design by Chip Butzko

Library of Congress Cataloging-in-Publication Data
Welcome to the board! : an orientation for the new health care trustee
         / Health Research and Educational Trust of New Jersey.
                         p.   cm.
                 Includes bibliographical references.
                 ISBN 0-7879-5740-2 (paperback)
                 1. Hospital trustees.   2. Health facilities—Administration.
         I. Health Research and Educational Trust of New Jersey.
                 [DNLM: 1. Trustees.   2. Hospital Administration.   WX 150 W442
         1999]
         RA971.W455   1999
         362.1'1'0684—dc21
         DNLM/DLC
         for Library of Congress   98-52682
                                         CIP

Printed in the United States of America

PB Printing   10 9 8 7 6 5

Contents

Health care is the most politically charged, volatile, erratic industry in America today. Take a look at how the health care industry has changed and how these changes have radically altered the role of the trustee and the traditional definition of health.

Every trustee who takes a seat at the hospital or health system board table takes on fundamental—and personal—responsibilities. In this chapter, we explore the individual trustee role in regard to time commitment, confidentiality, ethics, meeting attendance and participation, and ongoing education.

The most important work of any governing board is to determine the organization's mission, create its vision through strategic planning, and implement this plan through budget and program oversight. In this chapter we also examine the board's legal and fiduciary responsibilities.

Board and Committee Structures 47

While local hospital boards remain important, there are now health care system, regional, advisory, and foundation boards. We look at the roles and responsibilities of each type of board and consider such issues as credentialing for board members and physician membership.

Board Operations 55

All board members must remain current on best practices to fulfill the functions entrusted to them. Take an information-filled stroll through the breadth of board roles and responsibilities, such as strategic planning, executive hiring and performance review, board self-assessment, financial oversight, community accountability, quality assurance, and advocacy.

Glossary and Abbreviations 73

The language of health care has changed significantly. This glossary provides terminology, abbreviations, initialisms, and acronyms commonly used by professionals involved in the hospital and health care industry. It has been designed to help trustees navigate through terms related to medicine, finance, and insurance.

About the Trustee Institute

The Health Research and Educational Trust of New Jersey (HRET), the not-for-profit educational and research affiliate of the New Jersey Hospital Association (NJHA), launched the HRET Trustee Institute in the fall of 1996. Made possible by a grant from the Fannie E. Rippel Foundation and funding from the American Hospital Association and the New Jersey Hospital Association, the institute was charged with developing a broad array of educational programming and resources for hospital and health system trustees.

The institute has created a classroom without walls designed to fit into busy lifestyles and enable today's trustees to learn at their own pace and on their own schedule. Institute products include: a trustee Web site; a series of videotapes and audiotapes featuring noted governance experts and health care trustees; regional symposia and interactive video conferences; and this orientation guide for hospital and health system trustees.

For more information on the Trustee Institute and its programs and resources, contact the institute at 609-275-4145, or point your Internet browser to the Trustee Institute on NJHA's Web site at *http://www.njha.com.*

Acknowledgments

Welcome to the Board! is the culmination of a three-year project of the Trustee Institute and the American Hospital Association. The institute acknowledges and thanks the New Jersey Hospital Association Council on Hospital Governance for its support and guidance and the following members of the Trustee Institute Advisory Committee who shaped its focus and content:

Barbara Beeker
Cathedral Healthcare System

Marcia D. Corrigan
The Valley Hospital

Alice Holzapfel
Elizabeth General Medical Center

Jack Homan
The Memorial Hospital of Salem County

John S. Makel
Alliance Memorial Hospital of Burlington County

Martha Mason
Shore Memorial Hospital

Robert Mill
Bayonne Hospital

Msgr. Harrold A. Murray
St. Francis Lifecare Corp., Inc.

Carol Paul
Atlantic Health System

Earle Peterson, DVM
JFK Medical Center

Judith E. Thomas
Chestnut Hill HealthCare

Special thanks to governance consultant Keith Pryor, The Diversified Search Companies, Philadelphia, for sharing his expertise; AHA's Joe Isaacs and Richard Bogue for their excellent advice and counsel; NJHA's Charlene Shapiro and Debby Hoffman for their leadership role in the institute; and Shari Mycek and NJHA's communications department, who produced this readable guide in partnership with AHA Press.

Foreword

As a trustee, you can be among the health care field's greatest strengths. You can help guide the long-term directions of your hospital or health system. You can supply the critical strategic balance that ensures both that the organization's goals are strongly supported and that the community's needs are well met. You make certain that the organization meets or exceeds all the regulatory and operating requirements—that the organization is in compliance. You play a key role in evaluating and overseeing the quality of the caregivers who practice in your organization. You can help your management team achieve excellent personal and organizational performance. And you often do it all as a volunteer in service to the community.

But trustees can also be weaknesses. Where trustees and the organization's administrative leadership are divided, or when trustees play a wholly passive role, governance can't be effective. If trustees end up too involved in issues of management and operations, or in the delicate relationship between the medical staff and the administration, they will have a harder time keeping their eyes on the larger, more strategic issues. Sometimes trustees doze, while organizational values and practices become dusty, or worse.

Here is my plea to you. Add strength to the mission of your hospital or health system. Pursue a vision. Be true to the mission. Take an active role in governance, but understand and be explicit where governance ends and management begins. Invest in learning about the context of health care. Bring your rich experience and your position of community leadership to the board and its deliberations. Establish and maintain a positive, productive, and supportive relationship with the organization's management. Excellence is everyone's goal.

Your journey to becoming a source of strength will be rich with learning and education. What does it mean to govern? What is excellence in health care governance? What are the most important opportunities and threats in health care? For your organization? What should be your organization's long-term strategy? These and other questions confront you as you accept the challenges of health care governance. *Welcome to the Board! An Orientation for the New Health Care Trustee* will help you begin answering these and other questions.

We are grateful that you and the other leaders on your governance team have chosen *Welcome to the Board!* as the first step in your journey toward governance excellence. Welcome to the board! Thank you for your commitment. Become our greatest strength.

Richard J. Davidson
President, American Hospital Association

When it came time for the NJHA/HRET Trustee Institute and the American Hospital Association to produce a resource for trustees of hospitals and health care systems, we were faced with an unprecedented challenge. We knew there was a need to provide trustees with an understanding of the rapidly evolving and complex health care environment and the changing duties and responsibilities of governance. In this fast-paced, visually oriented society—where few of us have time to linger over a cup of coffee, never mind a good book—we also knew that any resource aimed at truly guiding trustees into the new millennium had to be engaging and realistic. It had to be factual, yet challenging. And above all, it had to be timely.

Today's boards are undergoing major transformations at an unprecedented pace. While trustees across the state and nation are facing similar challenges, such as merger/acquisition, strategic planning, and building healthy communities, no two board rooms are addressing these issues simultaneously. Or in the same way.

In producing *Welcome to the Board!* we believe we have presented the key issues affecting hospital and health boards; best practices for approaching these issues; real-life, case-in-point examples; resources available for further reading; and pertinent discussion questions.

Being a trustee of a hospital or health care system has never been more challenging or potentially rewarding. The NJHA/HRET Trustee Institute, in cooperation with its sponsors—the Fannie E. Rippel Foundation and American Hospital Association—salutes the nation's health care trustees for your exceptional commitment to affordable, high-quality health care, the financial viability of your organizations, and improved community health. We look to your leadership in guiding the nation's health care providers into the twenty-first century and are confident that you will find this resource helpful in doing so—no matter where you may be in the process of board transformation and marketplace evolution.

Gary S. Carter, FACHE
President, New Jersey Hospital Association

Preface

As the twentieth century comes to a close, the profound changes experienced in the past 100 years are reflected in the many changes in health care. Advances in science, technology, and education; changes in lifestyles, employment, family structures, and transportation; transformations in the economy, the business world, and politics—all have affected the way health care is delivered. The one-building hospital has gone the way of the one-room schoolhouse. Today's hospital is a complex structure—a network of buildings, often linked only by microchips, serving patients throughout their life span in varying stages of wellness within and beyond the hospital's walls.

What has not changed, however, is that the hospital remains the community's most valuable and valued resource. Entering the new millennium, members of hospital governing boards, entrusted with the hospital's welfare, are faced with unparalleled challenges. Their role on the board calls for knowledgeable decision making during turbulent times, when even their own hospital and board may be undergoing dramatic change.

Governing boards must address the question of how to orient new board members and keep seasoned members well informed about the latest trends in health care and boardsmanship. Where to begin? Developed by the NJHA/HRET Trustee Institute and the American Hospital Association (AHA), *Welcome to the Board! An Orientation for the New Health Care Trustee* is designed to serve as the cornerstone of trustee education for the year 2000 and beyond. Seasoned and novice trustees alike will find the guide a solid foundation on which to build, as boards and their members evolve to meet health care's future.

Recognizing that every hospital and health care system is different, requiring governing structures that best suit the individual institution or system and the community it serves, *Welcome to the Board!* does not profess to offer the one "right" way to operate a hospital board. Rather, it guides trustees through the evolution of health care governance and shows how this evolution is reflected in individual member and full board responsibilities, board and committee structures, and board operations. Case examples illuminate critical points. "Points to Ponder" bring the information to the trustee's own hospital world and can be used as a checklist to assess trustee understanding of health care issues and board practices. These points can also be used to facilitate trustee discussion. Each section includes recommended readings to further one's knowledge in specific areas.

Board chairs and trustees are encouraged to use *Welcome to the Board!* as they prepare to move their boards and health care organizations forward into the twenty-first century. As the cornerstone for trustee education, it will lead readers to the Trustee Institute's other resources, including the Trustee Institute and AHA sites on the World Wide Web and audio- and videotapes that will complement the material found in this publication.

Introduction

Richard J. Bogue and Joseph C. Isaacs
Division of Trustee and Community Leadership
American Hospital Association

As a new board member, you are entering one of the world's most rewarding endeavors. Every day, the people who work for hospitals and health systems help people beset by disease and prevent sickness among those who are well. Both patients and caregivers may not always know it, but they depend on board members to keep health care organizations on track. While working as a board member, you will reap great rewards from overseeing an organization that maintains the physical, mental, emotional, and spiritual wellness of your fellow human beings. You will also be rewarded as you draw on some of humanity's most precious values in your decision making: access, accountability, integrity, excellence, leadership, pluralism, and responsibilities.[1]

Of course, you will learn that with these rewards come magnificent challenges. A well-known expert on health care governance wrote in 1990 that the "American hospital is arguably the most complex . . . organization in existence."[2] Health care is even more complex today. You will have much to learn, and so long as you remain committed to service as a board member, the need to learn will never end.

Welcome to the board! As we help you start your education for health care governance, we salute you and offer you this toast: May your rewards and challenges always be enriched by learning, and may the wisdom that you gain touch many lives!

1

What Is Governance?

To govern means to exercise responsible ownership on behalf of the organization's stakeholders.[3] In early 1999, about 85 percent of the nation's community hospitals were controlled by not-for-profit corporations or local governments (municipal, county, or state).* For these organizations, the most obvious stakeholders are patients, staff, physicians, and others who see the organization as a resource. In fact, every member of the community served by the organization holds some kind of stake in the organization, its performance, and its future.

The other 15 percent of community hospitals are operated through a for-profit form of corporation. Stockholders represent a special class of stakeholders who share in the financial interests of these organizations. But even here, governing bodies exercise their authority on behalf of a broad set of stakeholders. Staff, physicians, and vendors as well as current, past, and future patients and their advocates hold stakes in the organization's performance. In other words, no matter the corporate form of a health care organization, boards exercise responsible owner-

ship for many individuals and groups—for "communities."

This principle of responsible ownership on behalf of communities shows why governance is carried out by teams. In health care, the governance team is composed of the board and those others who participate in exercising ownership for key elements of the community, including top executives and physician leaders. In fact, health care governance has been described as a "three-legged stool," with the purpose of the organization (metaphorically, the seat) held stable and sound by the board, the administration, and physician leadership together.[4]

It is easy to see the appropriateness of the three-legged stool metaphor when you remember that many different interests must be balanced with each other for the organization to serve patients, staff, physicians, and future patients, and therefore to meet its purposes for existing. That's why governance is carried out by teams. Only rarely should board members act as individuals, although a board chair will be expected to act as an individual for some parts of that special role. Boards act as a

---

*Federal hospitals, including the military and veterans' systems, are not considered community hospitals. Their "community" is more exclusive, although the Department of Veterans Affairs health systems are experimenting with new forms of partnership and service structures that may make some of them community hospitals too.

collective body, not as a collection of individuals. This reflects the core governance challenge of advancing the mission of the organization while also acting on behalf of many different interests.

Understanding governance as responsible ownership on behalf of a community also shows that a board's role is very much about relationships. In fact, five key kinds of relationships define the context for the governance of today's health care organization:[5]

- Board-mission relationship
- Board-CEO relationship
- Board-physician entity relationships
- Board-board and board-trustee relationships
- Board-community relationships

Welcome to the Board! gives a lot of information and guidance about how to govern. Here in the introduction, we only set the stage. Three observations about these relationships, however, are especially

POINTS TO PONDER

➤ What core values guide your decision making for your organization?

➤ What are the most important functions of your organization?

➤ Of which communities is your organization a member?

➤ How does your governance team keep focused on accomplishing responsible ownership on behalf of the community? To accomplish this, how will your organization change in the future?

➤ What are the most important relationships for your organization? In the future, which organizations will be most important to your institution's ability to meet its mission?

important because they underlie virtually everything that health care boards are learning to do differently than they may have done in the past.

First, a health care organization today does not function independently of other health care institutions. Largely as a result of financial pressures in health care—but also as part of a global change in thinking about excellence in business practices—affiliations, alliances, networks, and systems have become part of every governing board's context for decision making.[6] Among other things, this means that boards sometimes best serve their organization's mission by relating with other boards. The complexity of all this also presents many opportunities for potential conflicts of interest, emphasizing the great care that individual trustees must take in their relationships with different organizations and individuals.

Second, health care organizations today are increasingly energized by new ways of working with the communities they serve. Improving the health and well-being of the community is typically the ultimate reason for the organization's existence. But serving a community health-focused vision and mission is not always the same as serving the organization. The table comparing five core principles of governance from the twentieth century with those of the twenty-first century brings this point home.

GOVERNANCE PRINCIPLES

Twentieth Century	Twenty-First Century
Preserve and protect the current order	Create the conditions for a new order to emerge
Define health care as complication management	Redefine health care in terms of disease management and community health
Be mission driven	Become vision and mission driven
Promote self-interest	Promote stewardship
Enable the organization	Empower the organization and the community

Adapted from Scott W. Goodspeed, *Community Stewardship: Applying the Five Principles of Contemporary Governance* (Chicago: American Hospital Publishing, Inc., 1997).

Third, health care organizations, today more than ever, need boards that work with the rest of the governance team to foster and empower both vision and mission. Almost everything you will read about health care will start by emphasizing how much rapid change health care organizations face—and for very good reasons. Given these changes, a high premium must be placed on vision and mission. Otherwise, the organization may find itself lost at sea, with no direction and no compass.

As a final note on "What Is Governance?" let us call upon Carolyn Lewis, a trustee for Greater Southeast Health System, Washington, D.C., and the first trustee ever to serve as chair of the board of the American Hospital Association. She eloquently captures the essence of governance as responsible ownership on behalf of the community: "If anything we're doing in the boardroom doesn't matter to the people outside the hospital, *then we're doing the wrong thing.*"[7]

The Health Care Environment

Making decisions without a solid sense of context begs for trouble, especially in a rugged and changing environment like health care. This is why everyone's book of advice on strategic planning starts with understanding the environment. As discussed later in *Welcome to the Board!*, the job with the most enduring impact is the board's participation in strategic planning. But honestly, all your most important jobs as a board member demand a good understanding of the environment.

The upshot is that an ongoing effort to understand the environment is essential for board members, rookies, and veterans alike. Here we introduce you to some of the context you'll face as a governing board member with a broad panorama of the health care environment.

The table on "Total U.S. Spending on Health Care" breaks this down into percentages for different spending sources. Notice that hospital inpatient spending now represents much less of the total than it did in 1980, while hospital outpatient spending has more than doubled. This trend is very significant and certain to continue. As more and more hospital services are delivered in an outpatient setting, what does this trend say to governance teams about the definition of the term *hospital?*

Today, the functions of governance are often allocated across different layers of organization, from hospital boards to system boards.

TOTAL U.S. SPENDING ON HEALTH CARE, 1980, 1996

Spending, by Type	1980	1996
Community hospital inpatient	30.1%	21.0%
Community hospital outpatient	4.5%	9.9%
Other hospitals (e.g., psychiatric, federal)	6.9%	3.8%
Skilled nursing facilities	7.1%	7.6%
Home health agencies	1.0%	2.9%
Physicians	18.3%	19.5%
Other (e.g., personal care, research, public health, net cost of insurance)	32.1%	35.3%

Source: Medicare Payment Advisory Commission, *Health Care Spending and the Medicare Program: A Data Book,* July 1998.

For example, hospital boards typically exercise authority over quality assurance and managed care contracting decisions, but system boards often exercise authority over major capital expenditures and CEO appointments. The bar chart shows the percentage of hospital boards that report to a higher authority. What should governance teams do to take today's multilayer decision making into account?

Managed care matters to your decision making about finances, quality of care, and strategy. According to the SMG Marketing Group, health maintenance organization (HMO) enrollment has more than doubled since 1988. The rapid growth of managed care has changed forever certain underlying assumptions about how health care is financed and delivered. Even locations that have not been directly affected much by managed care yet are being affected by the changes in these underlying assumptions. It has happened so fast that this rate of increase can't continue. But the upward trend is likely to continue and locations that have seen little managed care penetration so far should be expecting more in the not-too-distant future. A question board members face is: How do the realities of managed care balance with our goals for care management?

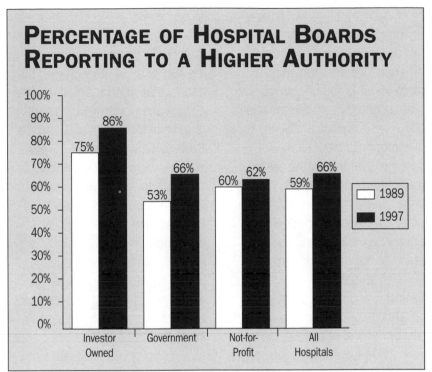

**PERCENTAGE OF HOSPITAL BOARDS
REPORTING TO A HIGHER AUTHORITY**

Legend: □ 1989 ■ 1997

Investor Owned: 75% (1989), 86% (1997)
Government: 53% (1989), 66% (1997)
Not-for-Profit: 60% (1989), 62% (1997)
All Hospitals: 59% (1989), 66% (1997)

Source: American Hospital Association and Ernst & Young, LLP, *Shining Light on Your Board's Passage to the Future* (Chicago: AHA/E&Y, 1997).

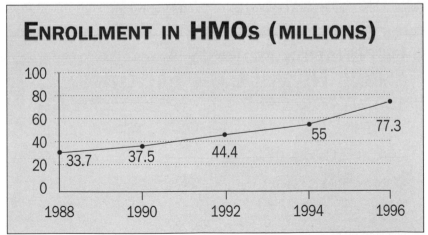

ENROLLMENT IN HMOS (MILLIONS)

1988: 33.7
1990: 37.5
1992: 44.4
1994: 55
1996: 77.3

Sources: Hoechst Marion Roussel Managed Care Digest Series, *HMO-PPO/Medicare-Medicaid Digest,* 1997; SMG Marketing Group, Inc. (data © 1997); and the Health Care Financing Administration.

Hospitals, physician groups, managed care organizations (MCOs), and other health care organizations are integrating in many ways. Environmental pressure increases both formal integration (consolidation) and voluntary integration (collaboration). But opportunities to improve performance for patients and for the organizations themselves are two other big reasons for integration. Governing well demands understanding not only your institution, but also its partners, potential partners, and competitors.

The many acquisitions of hospitals by national or regional chains have made the news over the past several years, giving the impression of a huge growth in system ownership of hospitals. There has been a recent increase, but it's not as large as the media would lead one to expect. For one thing, when chains have acquired hospitals, they have often done so by acquiring part or all of other chains. The central lesson behind acquisitions by systems is that while integration is a major trend in health care, centralized ownership is not the only way to accomplish integration.

It often seems that improved health and improved financial performance are mutually exclusive. A well-functioning health care governing body will face, over and over again, the challenge of balancing what's best for people's health and what's best for the organization's finances. A sign of excellence in health care governance might be discovering many ways to achieve both. Some examples have been proposed by the Centers for Disease Control as shown in the table on the next page.

INTEGRATION ACTIVITY AMONG HEALTH CARE FACILITIES

	Hospitals	MCOs	Group Practices
Joined a hospital or system	47%	32%	27%
Joined a physician network	23%	23%	63%
Formed equal partnerships	33%	42%	23%
Acquired by another entity	16%	23%	10%
Acquired another entity	26%	52%	29%

Source: *Hospitals & Health Networks,* August 5, 1997, p. 30.

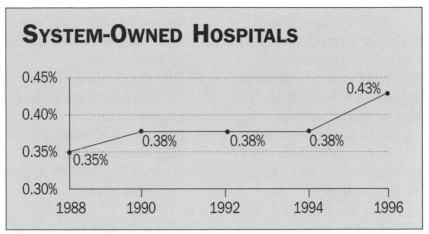

SYSTEM-OWNED HOSPITALS

0.45%
0.43%
0.40%
0.38%   0.38%   0.38%
0.35%
0.35%
0.30%
1988   1990   1992   1994   1996

Source: *Hospital Statistics,* Chicago: American Hospital Association, 1989–1997, and Healthcare InfoSource, Inc., 1998.

CENTERS FOR DISEASE CONTROL PREVENTION STATISTICS

If $1 is spent . . .	. . . delivering prenatal care to poorly educated, low-income women . . .	**. . . $3 are saved in just the child's first year of life.**
If $1 is spent . . .	. . . on effective hospital programs preventing nosocomial infections (infections acquired as a result of a hospital stay) . . .	**. . . $5 are saved.**
If $1 is spent . . .	. . . through measles, mumps and rubella (MMR) immunization programs . . .	**. . . $14 are saved.**
If $1 is spent . . .	. . . preventing just one in five new HIV infections . . .	**. . . $15 to $25 are saved.**

Source: Centers for Disease Control, *An Ounce of Prevention* (Atlanta: CDC, 1994).

There are ways to think strategically that will enable your governance team to face these and other major environmental trends in health care. The American Hospital Association board formally approved a future-oriented and systems-focused strategic vision for health care in 1992. This Community Care Network^{SM} vision shows one way of adapting to fundamental shifts in the health care environment.*

The Community Care Network (CCN) vision encourages collaboration among the many organizations throughout a community that can contribute to an improved health care system. Partners in these efforts often include insurers, business alliances, schools, religious organizations, social service agencies, public health departments, local governments, and community-based organizations, as well as health systems, hospitals, long-term care facilities, clinics, and physician groups. Evolving CCNs are guided by five goals:

1. Increasing access and coverage
2. Restoring public trust and enhancing accountability to populations and communities
3. Imbuing the health care system with a focus on population and community health
4. Improving coordination among the many parts of the health care system
5. Improving the efficiency and effectiveness of health care delivery as a system rather than a collection of parts

The CCN vision is one way of thinking that enables strategic adaptation to the environmental shifts mentioned earlier, as well as other shifts affecting the delivery of health care. The changes in thinking enabled by the CCN vision are summarized in the table on the next page.

Many health care organizations have already adapted ideas like the CCN vision to their local circumstances as a way of being strategic about the environmental changes happening in health care. Whatever the source, no matter what you call it, your governance team needs both an understanding of the environment and a vision to be able to design a good long-term strategy for your organization and your community. We offer you our very best wishes in this, your core challenge.

---

*Community Care Network, Inc., uses the name Community Care Network^{SM} as its service mark and reserves all rights.

CHANGES IN ORGANIZATIONAL THINKING ENABLED BY THE CCN VISION

Old Thinking	New Thinking
Disease oriented	Health oriented
Fragmentation	Integration
Competing institutions	Shared power and collaboration
Physicians as adversaries	Physicians as partners
Limited financial risk	Broad financial risk
Independent agent	Part of a community of social agents
Accountable to governing bodies	Accountable to community as well
Individual patients	An entire population
Hospitals and health care systems	Organizers and joiners of community care networks

Source: American Hospital Association, *Transforming Health Care Delivery: Toward Community Care Networks* (Chicago: American Hospital Association, 1993).

Who's Who in Health Care

Health care in the United States, viewed from any vantage point, can be seen as a huge network of relationships. The purpose of this section is to give you a quick overview of some of the many important organizations and agencies that make up this network.

Looking at different kinds of relationships is a useful way to make sense out of health care's large, complex network. A simple approach that an institution may use divides other organizations into collaborators and competitors. That approach may be too simple, however, and many leaders are learning how to find zones of collaboration around community health and other opportunities even with their competitors.

A more useful way of organizing the relationships of your organization is to discuss them as *task relationships, regulatory relationships,* or *political relationships.* We've used this approach to introduce you to some of the organizations that you will find to be most important to your institution.

Task Relationships

Task relationships are those that involve your organization directly in meeting its primary functions. The primary functions of your hospital or health system include some or all of the following:

1. Providing patient care
2. Sponsoring health education and preventive interventions for the community
3. Training health practitioners
4. Participating in medical research
5. Providing laboratories and other medical services
6. Providing management services for other organizations[8]

This list indicates some of the organizations that have task relationships with yours. When thinking chiefly about patient care, for example, your organization's task relationships are with a variety of other providers, payers, patients, and suppliers.

Provider is a term often used in health care to refer generically to the many different kinds of organizations and individuals that deliver health services directly. Included are physician organizations and practice groups, your employees, nursing homes, other hospitals, home health agencies, visiting nurses associations, and laboratory services.

The term *payers* is often used in health care to refer to the many different organizations that pay for some or all of the functions of your organization (sometimes people identify the "purchasers" of care as a group distinct from payers). Payers include private insurance companies, self-insured companies, Medicare and Medicaid, fiscal intermediaries (companies that contract with Medicare or Medicaid to act as agents for the government's payments to your organization), and, to some extent, consumers.

Patients, of course, you know. But their families as well as their advocates, such as attorneys or clergy, also participate with your organization in the work of health care.

If you inquire about your organization's role in training health professionals, you may find a somewhat different set of organizations working with yours. For this function, your organization probably works with a medical school; agencies that certify health care professionals, such as the Board of Medical Examiners and state licensing agencies for physicians, nurses, and other health professionals; and perhaps the Area Health Education Center (AHEC). One of the board's key jobs is ensuring that procedures for quality control through physician credentialing are in place, and this may involve your organization with national and state agencies that collect and report information on practitioner performance, hospitals where they previously practiced, and physician specialty examination boards.

When you think about the other organizations your institution works directly with to advance health education and prevention, the list is a little different. In this case, it might or might not include any payers, but it is likely to include public health agencies, the school system, civic or social organizations, religious institutions, and the local media.

It will probably be useful to you to organize your thinking about the task relationships your institution has with other organizations by exploring its different functions. In this way, you not only gain a method for organizing your thoughts about a very complex network of organizations; but also you'll learn how to ask important strategic questions about why your institution does or does not have a working relationship with certain other organizations in your area.

Regulatory Relationships

A second set of relationships that defines the U.S. health care system can be called a regulatory set. Health care is highly regulated in the United States. Many organizations and agencies that rarely or never work directly with your organization have important roles in establishing the rules for its operation.

One discussed at some length later in *Welcome to the Board!* is the Joint Commission for the Accreditation of Healthcare Organizations (JCAHO). The JCAHO is a private agency that serves the public interest by establishing standards for facilities and for management and governance practices and processes, traditionally to ensure high-quality patient care.

The National Committee on Quality Assurance (NCQA), a younger organization than the JCAHO but also private, focuses more attention on quality of care for populations through the development and use of outcomes measures. The NCQA's measures, which are called HEDIS (Health Plan Employer Data and Information Set), are especially suited to the managed care environment and for use by self-insured employers.

The Foundation for Accountability (FACCT) is even newer than the NCQA, and emphasizes outcome measures especially designed to be useful to consumers. Your organization's pursuit of accreditation is voluntary, although JCAHO or NCQA accreditation may be required for certification from some payers.

Accreditation is an important means by which your organization can periodically assess itself against industry standards and demonstrate its high quality to payers and the public.

Just touching some of the major private initiatives on quality introduces you to three initialisms within three paragraphs. Learning and using initialisms and acronyms is essential to following many conversations in health care. But as a board member you have the prerogative, and often the duty, to make sure you are given materials to help you understand what these organizations are and do without confusing jargon. This enables you to engage your judgment and wisdom. But it also enables you to help others see how health care issues can be better communicated to patients and communities.

There are many government agencies that belong to the regulatory set of relationships for your organization. The U.S. Department of Health and Human Services (DHHS) oversees a vast array of public health and health care functions. Among the agencies of DHHS is the Health Care Financing Administration (HCFA), which may be the most important regulatory agency in health care. HCFA oversees the Medicare program and works with the states to oversee Medicaid.

Some organizations that have regulatory relationships with your own organization—such as the Agency for Health Care Policy and Research (AHCPR) and the Congressional Budget Office (CBO)— conduct and support research that informs the decision making of those who set the rules. Other organizations, such as the Food and Drug Administration (FDA) and the Office of the Inspector General (OIG) of the U.S. Department of Health and Human Services, also have policy enforcement roles. Fortunately, many government agencies have names that describe accurately their purview. The glossary includes the names and acronyms of government agencies that help set and enforce the rules and regulations for how your organization works.

In health care today, there is not much push for major legislation at the federal level that would fundamentally change many basic rules about how your organization meets its functions. Of course, this lack of a push for major change may be temporary. But for now it appears likely that federal policy makers will enact only incremental changes over the next few years. These could include creating new rules and regulations surrounding patients' rights and consumer protections, efforts to reduce Medicare payments to providers, and other changes to ensure long-term solvency for Medicare. You might also expect to see modest, incremental expansions of Medicaid or Medicare to address the uninsured, especially among children.

An era of incrementalism in health care regulation also means that state-level rule makers are having an especially large impact on health care, at least for the time being. Important government offices in your state include the Insurance Commissioner, the Attorney General, licensing agencies for hospitals and health professions, the Medicaid program, and the Public Health Department. Over the next several years, various states will be considering changes to Medicaid funding and eligibility, patients' rights and consumer protection, and rules governing changes in hospital ownership or control.

While states are currently at center stage in making new rules about health care, a critical barrier to major changes in health care financing at the state level is the federal Employee Retirement and Security Income Act of 1974 (ERISA). This act prohibits states "from requiring all employers to offer health insurance, from regulating or taxing self-insured plans, from taxing or assessing surcharges on employer welfare benefit plans, and from mandating that specific benefits be covered by employer health plans."[9] Learning about ERISA's influence in health care will introduce you to many of today's key issues, including integration among providers; relationships among employers, health insurers, and providers; and relationships between payers and providers that assume some level of financial risk.

Political Relationships

Forming a bridge between the task relationships, which your organization exercises regularly to do its work, and the regulatory relationships, which determine the rules for your organization's work, is a political set of relationships. It is the ebb and flow of public and legislative opinion that sets up the rules, both mandatory and voluntary, that shape how your hospital or health system works.

As a community leader, you may already know a lot about politics at the local, state, and federal levels. But you may not have given much thought to the tremendous potential you represent as an advocate for health care in the political arena.

You may be volunteering your effort as a health care board member. You are not going to make decisions that benefit you at the expense of your organization's purposes. Many policy makers will understand that you serve in the community's interest and, as a result, you can be an especially powerful advocate.

HEALTH CARE GOVERNANCE AT THE MILLENIUM: KEY STATISTICS

	Hospitals (N = 2,079)	Health Systems (N = 126)
Percent of boards reporting to higher boards	• 41% report to a board or management of a parent holding company • 34% are not responsible to a higher authority • 16% report to a unit of state, county, or municipal government • 9% report to a religious, university, or other board	N/A
Average number of voting board members	13.2	17.8
Average number of female members	3.1	4.5
Average number of physician members	3.1	3.9
Average number of ethnic minority members	2.4	3.2
Average number of members over 70 years of age	2.2	2.4

HEALTH CARE GOVERNANCE AT THE MILLENIUM (CONTINUED)		
Top five board member selection criteria	• Values consistent with hospital • Community leadership (tie) • Financial/business acumen • Strategic planning/visioning • Time availability • Political influence	• More than 50% of boards recruit members based on professional expertise or discipline, especially clinical or health care delivery expertise and/or community knowledge. • 25% of boards develop a comprehensive expertise profile in advance and maintain a list of prospective members who fit the profile.
Top five CEO performance evaluation criteria	• Hospital financial performance • Vision and other leadership qualities • Physician relations and integrations • Fulfillment of strategic plan • Mission fulfillment • Employee relations (tie)	• Fulfillment of strategic plan • Financial performance • Vision and other leadership qualities • Mission fulfillment • Physician relations and integration
Top five types of data most commonly reported to the board on a regular basis	• Operating statistics • Financial statement performance • Budget performance • Capital planning • Patient satisfaction surveys	• Budget performance • Financial statement performance • Capital planning • Operating statistics • Employee attitude surveys
Top three priorities for board improvement	• Education • Medical staff alignment • Measurement and evaluation	• Physician alignment • Leadership effectiveness • Education

Source: American Hospital Association, 1997 Governance Survey.

As you gain experience as a board member, you should work with your administration and the rest of the board on ways that your governance team can participate in political relationships. Many of the national and state associations with which your organization is affiliated, such as the American Hospital Association and your state association, provide excellent opportunities for advocacy by board members. When you get involved in this way, you help shape the rules. You also help enable your organization to serve its community as well as it possibly can.

References

1. American Hospital Association. Statement of Values (Chicago: American Hospital Association, 1998).

2. Mary K. Totten, James E. Orlikoff, and C. M. Ewell. *The Guide to Governance for Hospital Trustees* (Chicago: American Hospital Association, 1990).

3. Richard J. Umbdenstock, Winifred M. Hageman, and B. Amundson. "The Five Critical Areas for Effective Governance of Not-for-Profit Hospitals," *Frontiers of Health Services Management* (Winter 1990).

4. Stephen M. Shortell. "New Directions in Hospital Governance," *Frontiers of Health Services Management* (Spring 1989).

5. James E. Orlikoff and Mary K. Totten. *The Future of Health Care Governance* (Chicago: American Hospital Publishing, Inc., 1996), pp. 29–37.

6. A. D. Kaluzny, Howard S. Zuckerman, and Thomas C. Ricketts III, eds. *Partners for the Dance: Forming Strategic Alliances in Health Care* (Chicago: Health Administration Press, 1995).

7. Richard J. Umbdenstock and Richard J. Bogue. *Trustees and the Integration of Community Health Care* (Chicago: Health Research and Educational Trust, 1993), p. 11.

8. William C. Cockerham. *Medical Sociology,* 7th ed. (Upper Saddle River, NJ: Prentice-Hall, 1998).

9. D. F. Beatrice. "States and Health Care Reform: The Importance of Implementation," in *Strategic Choices for a Changing Health Care System,* Stuart H. Altman and Uwe E. Reinhardt, eds. (Chicago: Health Administration Press, 1996), pp. 183–206.

Evolution of Health Care and Governance

Health care, it has been said, is the most politically charged, volatile, erratic industry in America today. In weathering the changes, those most deeply entrenched in leading health care delivery—senior executives, trustees, and clinical leaders—have two choices. They can continue the status quo and hope that the storm blows over. Or, more realistically, they can put up their umbrellas and learn how to work in the rain.

The driving force behind the rain—which in some parts of the country is pouring in blinding sheets; in other parts only beginning to trickle—is managed health care and the dramatic changes in reimbursement associated with it.

As managed care increases its market share, hospitals are in the quandary of becoming expense centers as opposed to revenue centers. This is a dramatic shift from the days when every inpatient day, every test ordered, and every clinical procedure performed generated revenue for the hospital. In many communities, hospitals—as single organizations—can no longer survive without joining with like, and unlike, health care entities such as rehabilitation centers, long-term care facilities, hospices, and home care units to form integrated delivery systems to spread risk and capture efficiencies across the continuum of care.

This is, of course, a dramatic shift. At the beginning of the twentieth century the average life span was 45 years. Hospitals, whose sole purpose was to treat the sick and injured, were built in every town. In combination with improved public health they contributed significantly to improved health status and, by the eve of the new millennium, had lengthened the average life span to 78 years.

As former Surgeon General C. Everett Koop often points out: "During the first half of the twentieth

19

century we were dealing with diseases—rheumatic fever, polio, smallpox—over which we had little control." The use of vaccinations has virtually eradicated such in-the-wrong-place-at-the-wrong-time contagious diseases so that now we are left largely with lifestyle-related illnesses: heart disease, cancer, and HIV/AIDS to name a few. The National Institutes of Health reports that half of all health problems are caused by behaviors such as smoking, excessive use of alcohol, and poor diet, all of which are preventable.

During the 1980s and 1990s, as the percentage of the Gross Domestic Product (GDP) spent on health care continued to escalate to its current level of nearly 15 percent, it became increasingly evident that the American public could not

WHAT CONSTITUTES HEALTH?

When the Healthcare Forum surveyed the American public about "health" and factors that would make their lives healthier, little was said about hospitals or physicians or the health care industry. Instead, citizens ranked the following as critical determinants:

- ❏ Low crime rate . . . . (73 percent)
- ❏ Good place to bring up children. . . . . (73 percent)
- ❏ Low level of child abuse. . . . . (72 percent)
- ❏ Not afraid to walk late at night . . . . (71 percent)
- ❏ Good schools . . . . (71 percent)
- ❏ Strong family life . . . . (70 percent)
- ❏ High environmental quality . . . . (65 percent)
- ❏ Good jobs and economy. . . . . (64 percent)
- ❏ Excellent race relations . . . . (57 percent)
- ❏ Low teenage pregnancy . . . . (57 percent)
- ❏ Low homelessness . . . . (55 percent)
- ❏ Low infant mortality. . . . . (54 percent)
- ❏ Affordable housing . . . . (47 percent)
- ❏ Recycling efforts/programs . . . . (42 percent)
- ❏ Strong religious life . . . . (42 percent)
- ❏ Good infrastructure . . . . (40 percent)
- ❏ Public space to meet friends . . . . (36 percent)
- ❏ Day care facilities . . . . (35 percent)
- ❏ Public transportation . . . . (33 percent)

afford to pay the price of treating lifestyle diseases. A slashing effect followed as businesses, third-party payers, and even the federal government began drawing hard lines as to what they were willing—or, in most cases, not willing—to pay for health care. Today, repercussions continue with an added challenge facing health leaders: the future of entitlement programs. No longer can health leaders take for granted that entitlement programs, including Medicare and Medicaid reimbursement, will be available to the extent they are now. Institutions must prepare today to be less dependent tomorrow on the revenues from these programs.

Ultimately, progressive health care organizations, along with private industry and insurers, will work with other health care providers and communities to redefine health: not as the absence of disease, but as the well-being of individuals, families, and entire communities. Increasingly, health care professionals around the world are seeing behavioral change (that is, attitudes regarding smoking, drinking alcohol, substance abuse, use of seat belts, and so on) as a highly effective use of health care funds.

POINTS TO PONDER

➤ What are three main challenges/issues your board is facing, and how well equipped is your board to address them?

➤ Do you have the composition, structure, and information needed to address these issues? What's missing?

➤ How does your board define health? How does your community define health?

➤ What strategies and funding mechanisms are in place to support the hospital/health system's role in improving health and fostering needed coalition building among various stakeholders?

Governance Changes

These transitions in health care have altered, and in many ways overhauled, the role of the trustee. When hospitals were first formed in the 1700s, "boards of managers, trustees and governors" were selected from pools of wealthy merchants, bankers, lawyers, and political leaders for two reasons: (1) they had a lot of money to donate to the hospital or (2) they were connected to individuals who had a lot of money. Their role was largely philanthropic.

Today's boards, however, play a dramatically different role from their predecessors. Money and securing the organization's bottom line are, of course, still important. But the financial environment is much different from years ago. In a time of diminishing resources, continuing government regulation, and increased competition, the fiduciary responsibility implied in the definition of the title *trustee* has even greater implications. Ultimately, the board is responsible for the oversight of hospital finances and other operations. For many boards, the continued viability of their institutions is at stake, and the outcome will be determined by their ability to identify and generate new sources of capital.

But today's boards also must carefully balance their fiduciary responsibilities with a broader mission to serve their communities. When reviewing its organization's mission statement and the health care needs of its community, a board should pose three basic questions regarding the addition or elimination of services. Is there a need for this service? Is this a financially feasible program? If the program is important but apparently not financially viable, then a third question should be raised: What can we do to meet the need?

Along with attempts to streamline services, eliminate duplication, and provide more cost-effective health care, boards are also choosing partners in care—affiliating, consolidating, and merging with former competitors. With such partnerships comes the need to pay attention to antitrust issues, which in the past were not prominent on the board agenda.

Today, even boards themselves are different in composition and structure. Where there used to be only a single hospital board, there are now system boards, regional boards, local boards, and advisory boards—all with roles and responsibilities. Perhaps the greatest challenge to governance is the need to streamline decision-making processes and eliminate outmoded structures to foster timely, informed decisions that will move the organization forward.

"Once you get on a hospital or health system board, you get hooked because of the magnitude of the decisions you make," says

---

CASE IN POINT

Memorial Health System: This South Bend, Indiana, hospital began doing "plunges"—visits into various neighborhoods—several years ago as a way to reconnect with its community. It now conducts three to four plunges per year during which participants meet directly with the people. "We don't want to talk to the executive directors of the programs. We want to talk to the real people—to hear the real-life stories, "says Phil Newbold, president and CEO. Take "Doris" for example. Although her neighborhood block has been relatively stable, it has been showing increasing signs of deterioration and unrest. Pressed to describe the trouble, Doris notes that she "did hear gunshots last night. Again. I get sick and tired of hearing gunshots."

Doris explains that the narrow alleys running between the bungalow-style homes are a breeding ground for drinking, drug deals, loud cars, profanity, and the shots she hears ring out at night. "I'd love to close the alley off," she says. "But I don't have $250 to do it with."

"This [plunge] opened my eyes to the complexities people go through because our worlds are so different," says Memorial Trustee Richmond Calvin. "To me, these were nothing more than cute little alleyways. I never thought of the danger."

(Excerpted from *Trustee,* vol. 50, no. 9, October 1997, by permission. Copyright 1997, American Hospital Publishing, Inc.)

Frontline governance—like Memorial's plunges—is what's needed for the trustee of tomorrow, according to Joe Isaacs, vice president of Trustee and Community Leadership for the AHA Center for Health Care Leadership. "Health care in the future is going to be community-based," he says. "True understanding of the community can be obtained only by breaking down the board room walls and exposing trustees directly to life experiences."

Winifred Hageman, an independent governance consultant in Seattle and former trustee of the American Hospital Association. Certainly the demands of today's health care industry make a trustee's job a lot tougher than when it was a surefire ticket to the cocktail party circuit. Sometimes the responsibilities and demands on intellectual and emotional capital are exhausting. But for trustees participating in transforming their health care facilities and community, the results and benefits are rewarding. "The trustee is there to make the hospital accountable to the public," says William W. Mance Jr., a trustee at McDowell Hospital in Marion, North Carolina. "When I first started on the board, my primary responsibility was to the hospital. The hospital was where you cured sickness, not where you provided health. Today, we're talking about what we can do to improve the health of the community."

In balancing fiduciary responsibilities with the mission to improve community health, futurist Leland Kaiser advocates that boards set aside up to 10 percent of the organization's bottom line for community-based initiatives aimed at preventing illness and improving lifestyles. Hospitals have always set aside capital to some degree, but typically the "return" to the community has been in the form of a new hospital wing, parking garage, or medical equipment. "It seems that the programs and services that can truly improve the health and well-being of communities are not reimbursable by third-party payers," says Kaiser. "And so, health leaders must accept that accountability and provide for the community services not reimbursed."

The concept is called tithing. And in South Bend, Indiana, the board of Memorial Health System has had a tithing policy for several years now. According to CEO Phil Newbold, 10 percent is set aside to fund new services or program needs identified through community "plunges" (visits into neighborhoods). "Tithing sets aside the resources and takes away the argument of what contributions should be made in a given year," says Newbold. "Good or bad year—10 percent is prefunded."

RECOMMENDED READING

EVOLUTION OF HEALTH CARE AND GOVERNANCE

COFFEY, RICHARD J., KATE M. FENNER, AND SHERYL L. STOGIS. "Emerging Health and Social Systems," in *Virtually Integrated Health Systems: A Guide to Assessing Organization Readiness and Strategic Partners* (San Francisco: Jossey-Bass, 1997), pp. 1–26. BOOK CHAPTER.

ORLIKOFF, JAMES E. "From Hospital to Health System Governance," *Healthcare Executive,* vol. 12, no. 5, September-October 1997, pp. 14–18. ARTICLE.

PERSING, VIRGINIA, AND TRISH KROTOWSKI. *Celebrating Innovative Leadership in Healthcare* (U.S.: Windsor Publications in cooperation with the New Jersey Hospital Association, 1993). [ISBN 0-89781-470-3]. BOOK.

ROSENBERG, CHARLES E. "A Careful Oversight: Reshaping Authority," in *The Care of Strangers: The Rise of America's Hospital System* (New York: Basic Books, 1987), pp. 262–85. BOOK CHAPTER.

SACHS, MICHAEL A. "Managed Care: The Next Generation," *Frontiers of Health Services Management,* vol. 14, no. 1, Fall 1997, pp. 3–26. ARTICLE.

UMBDENSTOCK, RICHARD J. *So You're on the Hospital Board!* 4th ed. (Chicago: American Hospital Publishing, Inc., 1992). [ISBN 1-55648-095-4]. BOOK.

Individual Trustee Responsibilities

As hospital trustee Carolyn B. Lewis was once heard to say, "If anything we're doing in the board room doesn't matter to the people outside the hospital, then we're doing the wrong thing."

Trustees who take seats at the hospital or health system board table bring along a fundamental responsibility to care for the organization as if it were their own—and to represent not their own personal interests or agendas, but the interests and agendas of the owners of the organization.

"Board members," says John Carver, author of *Boards That Make a Difference*, "cannot carry out their responsibilities without determining exactly whom they represent. And how their constituency can be heard." Defining ownership, however, can be tricky. In the case of not-for-profit organizations, for example, the true owners of the hospital or health system are not the administrators or physicians, or even the patients. Rather, the owners are members of the community at large.

Successfully carrying out the role of trustee—representing the owners' wants and needs versus merely serving as a rubber-stamp approval mechanism for the organization—means real work. "Sometimes it seems like being a trustee gets harder all the time," says trustee William W. Mance Jr.

So why do so many trustees serve on hospital and health system boards? Where does the satisfaction come from? And what keeps them productive and willing to serve in an often chaotic and always challenging position?

To many, it's simple: "I'm making a difference," notes Paul McKee, vice chairman of BJC Health System, St. Louis. "If I didn't believe I was making a difference, I'd be out of there this afternoon."

Making a difference does not come without a price tag on personal time and energy. Every trustee must take time to examine and understand the expectations and personal responsibilities associated with the job as they relate to time, ethics, confidentiality, conflict of interest, meeting attendance and participation, ongoing education, and the securing of appropriate information necessary to make sound business decisions.

WHY ARE THERE TRUSTEES?

The existence of hospital and health system boards is required by law, but fulfilling a legal obligation is not the trustees' sole purpose. More important is their moral obligation to represent their organization's owners and uphold their trust. Three leading governance experts comment:

From Keith Pryor, The Diversified Search Companies, Philadelphia: "When trustees understand that their job is to represent the owners of their organization, and when they define exactly who those owners are, their jobs become a lot clearer. They understand that their purpose is not to sit and approve staffs' wish list, but instead to represent what their owners want—and need—from the organization."

From John Carver, author of *Boards That Make a Difference:* "In many cases, boards learn to speak staff language, use staff acronyms and become involved in internal organization issues. And this understandable, intense identification with staff detracts from their being trusteeship driven. The mechanisms of board work must be designed to remind the board that its rightful identify is with the owners—not the staff."

From James E. Orlikoff, co-author of *The Future of Health Care Governance:* "When I ask most boards of not-for-profit organizations who owns the organization, I get blank stares. A lot of governance problems stem from boards that don't remind themselves they are accountable to the community and hold the organization's assets in trust for the community."

POINTS TO PONDER

➤ Who are the "owners" of your organization? How do you know if you're fulfilling your obligation to them? How do you keep them informed of your progress and challenges?

➤ Can you commit the amount of time needed to do your job as trustee?

➤ Do you adhere to the highest code of ethics? Do you follow confidentiality and conflict-of-interest standards? Are these established in your bylaws and policies? Are you covered by directors' and officers' liability insurance? Do you understand what this insurance entails?

Time, Attendance, and Participation

To say that responsible governance takes time is obviously an understatement; for many, it means dropping other commitments altogether. And the rewards aren't necessarily doled out in the form of money, benefits, or even gratitude. While some hospitals and health systems are beginning to compensate board members, trusteeship remains largely a volunteer effort, and individuals serving as trustees must do so out of a genuine commitment to their community. While the job should not take every waking hour, trustees should be prepared to dedicate a substantial amount of time to it.

Regular attendance at board meetings is certainly expected of trustees. In fact, failure to attend meetings can result in dismissal from many boards. But even perfect attendance is not enough; trustees must also be prepared and active. They must review board materials prior to meetings and, most important, participate in board discussions. Governance expert Keith Pryor contends that health care boardrooms throughout the country are simply too quiet. Not enough questions are being asked, and trustees may not always have access to the information necessary to make informed decisions.

Before trustees can begin tackling any of the big picture, health reform issues that ultimately need to be addressed, they must first start talking and asking questions.

Ethics

As keepers of the hospital's or system's mission and as policy makers for the institution, trustees are expected to exhibit the highest integrity and ethical behavior.

Conflict of Interest

Board members must be aware of the organization's conflict-of-interest policy and alert the chair of any potential conflicts in a timely manner. Most hospitals require that trustees in conflict of interest not vote on the related issue. Many boards go a step further, stating that trustees in conflict cannot be in the room for discussion of the issue. Some call for written ballots when a conflict exists, even if the trustee in conflict is not present. Practically all health care organizations now require trustees to sign an acknowledgment asserting they have read and understand the conflict-of-interest policy.

Confidentiality

Most trustees are required by their board to sign a personal confidentiality statement signifying that they agree to keep confidential—during and after service—all information

---

CASE IN POINT

Liability: In a Florida case, senior executives at Cape Coral Hospital were charged with fraud and misappropriation of hospital funds, bringing trustee loyalty and the duty of appropriate oversight into question. To date, liability for such actions has fallen only on those trustees who directly profited, but independent trustees who are not vigilant in observing their duties of care and loyalty could be increasingly held responsible. Not-for-profit boards need to pay more attention to national developments and potentially important distinctions in applicable state law.

CASES IN POINT

Quality of Information: Advocate Health Care System calls it a "dashboard." Dartmouth-Hitchcock calls it an "instrument panel." Henry Ford calls it a "balanced scorecard." But all these terms mean virtually the same thing—presenting information in a brief report that gives trustees a broad, multidimensional view of how their organization is doing. "Trustees who don't get information on critical measures of performance in a form they can understand are deluding themselves if they think they know what's going on in their organization," says Barry S. Bader, governance consultant. "It's like driving a car," says fellow governance expert Keith Pryor. "You don't necessarily need to know how every mechanism works, but you do need to know how fast you're going, if you need oil. Trustees have a certain obligation to oversee financial performance but that doesn't mean they need to know how many bills were issued last month. The information they should monitor can fit on one page." Included on these one-page dashboard reports are measures of financial, quality, market, and operational performance. Data are incorporated from financial statements as well as from clinical outcomes and benchmarking.

(Adapted from *Trustee,* vol. 50, no 4, April 1997, by permission. Copyright 1997, American Hospital Publishing, Inc.)

Ongoing Education: "Our board feels strongly about trustee qualifications and the need for continuing education," says trustee Dorothy H. Mann in a 1996 issue of *Trustee* magazine. "We budget for that. Every trustee has an individual [education] budget and we encourage first-term trustees to identify training sessions. We also mentor; we assign first-term trustees with seasoned trustees. It's important for the board to be knowledgeable about the business we're in. Whether it's a for-profit or not-for-profit organization, the critical governance issues are the same. It's important to keep up with the changes in the industry in order to be flexible, nimble and clear about strategies and tactics. There's always more than one way to accomplish our goals."

(Excerpted from *Trustee,* vol. 49, no.10, November/December 1996, by permission. Copyright 1996, American Hospital Publishing, Inc.)

pertaining to strategic plans, patients and the quality of their care, financial information, executive performance, medical recruitment, and real estate purchases. Essentially, confidentiality means you don't talk about it, says governance expert Keith Pryor. "You don't talk about it on your way out of the boardroom with a fellow trustee. You don't talk about it at dinner with your family. And you don't talk about it over lunch with your most trusted business partner."

Liability

As determined by statute, case law, and the fiduciary relationship to their organizations, trustees owe their institutions the twin duties of care and loyalty. The first requires a trustee to act in good faith and with as much care as a prudent businessperson would exercise in similar circumstances. Loyalty demands that trustees place the best interests of

POINTS TO PONDER

➤ Are you receiving easy-to-understand relevant information? Do you receive too little— or too much—information?

➤ Do you have a personal trustee reading library? Do you have access to one at your hospital or health system? Do you use it?

➤ Do you come prepared for board meetings? Do you actively participate and ask questions? Do you share your viewpoint?

➤ Does your board have formal, ongoing trustee education? Is it a specific line item in the hospital's/health system's budget? In what other ways do you stay current on health care and governance issues?

the corporation above personal concerns. "To both avoid liability and satisfy their duties, health care trustees must not only act in good faith, but be able to prove that they have done so," says Michael D. Phillips, a partner with the Cleveland law firm of Calfee, Halter & Griswold, LLP. "They must ask the right questions, aggressively seek out data on which to base their decisions, and generally adhere to the same level of care they would use in their own businesses."

Many hospitals and health care systems provide directors' and officers' (D&O) liability insurance. While such insurance is important to have, it must be understood that coverage does not protect against dereliction of duty.

Quality of Information

To make the difficult decisions that today's boards are pressed to make, trustees must have the right information in their hands so they understand the issues and can make intelligent and informed decisions. It is up to board members to ensure that they have this information. Trustees must speak up and let their CEOs know if they have too little—or too much—information. In many cases, board members are handed hefty management reports filled with a confusing jumble of numbers—often the same financial information given to COOs. And in this morass of paper and numbers, the information trustees need for making key decisions about their organization's future can be difficult to find. They should ask instead for a brief, one-page summary of key points.

Continuing Education

Most health care trustees—even those new to the board—should have an intelligible grasp of the trends shaping health care. After all, many trustees have dealt with mergers and integration, reengineering, and total quality improvement in their full-time day jobs as banking, manufacturing, and hospitality industry executives.

Unfortunately, many assume that health care trustees—in earning their seats at the board table—automatically know everything there is to know about issues such as managed care and graduate medical education, integrated delivery systems, Medicare reimbursement, and preserving the health of entire communities. Of course, such expectations are far from realistic. As health care continues to evolve at breakneck speed, even the most seasoned trustees are pressed to keep up-to-date. Yet many trustees—old and new alike—refrain from asking basic questions for fear of looking foolish.

Keeping up-to-date and understanding health care issues help trustees ask the questions they need to ask to keep their organizations moving forward. Continuing education opportunities at board meetings, off-site board retreats, mentoring programs, professional

Trustees have an obligation to keep up with issues in the health care field. One way to do that is by reading and creating a personal library. "Every trustee should prepare a little library at home, devote six inches of book-shelf space on being a trustee," says Keith Pryor. Many hospitals and health systems are often willing to donate "library" space for trustees.

A reasonable routine reading list would include:

➤ *The Wall Street Journal* or *The New York Times* for general health care issues
➤ An industry trade publication such as *Trustee* magazine
➤ Recommended articles on focused topics

Other recommendations include:

➤ *The Trustee Handbook for Health Care Governance* by James E. Orlikoff and Mary K. Totten
➤ *Boards That Make a Difference* by John Carver
➤ *The Future of Health Care Governance* by James E. Orlikoff and Mary K. Totten
➤ *Hospitals & Health Networks* magazine
➤ *Modern Healthcare* magazine
➤ *Health Forum Journal* magazine
➤ *Shining Light on Your Board's Passage to the Future* from AHA
➤ *Board-CEO Relationship Builders* from AHA
➤ *The Guide to Governance for Hospital and Health System Trustees* from AHA

workshops, seminars, and individual trustee training (including computer training) are critical to this process. Many hospitals and hospital associations now have Web sites, and the Internet can provide a wealth of information to trustees. Of course, old-fashioned reading is also a good source. Trustees are encouraged to create their own personal reading library dedicated to trustee issues.

RECOMMENDED READING

INDIVIDUAL TRUSTEE RESPONSIBILITIES

Purpose of Trustees

Carver, John. *Boards That Make a Difference: A New Design for Leadership in Nonprofit and Public Organizations,* 2d ed. (San Francisco: Jossey-Bass, 1997). [ISBN 0-78790-811-8]. BOOK.

Goodspeed, Scott W. *Community Stewardship: Applying the Five Principles of Contemporary Governance* (Chicago: American Hospital Publishing, Inc., 1997). [ISBN 1-55648-210-8]. BOOK.

"Governance," in *1998 Hospital Accreditation Standards* (Chicago: Joint Commission on Accreditation of Healthcare Organizations, 1998), pp. 215–19. [ISBN 0-86688-575-7]. BOOK CHAPTER.

Taylor, Barbara E., Richard P. Chait, and Thomas P. Holland, "The New Work of the Nonprofit Board," *Harvard Business Review*, vol. 74, no. 5, September-October 1996, pp. 36–46. ARTICLE.

Dashboard Indicators

Kennedy, Maggie. "Strategic Performance Measurement Systems: Next Step after Dashboards," *The Quality Letter,* vol. 7, no. 10, December 1995-January 1996, pp. 2–21. ARTICLE.

"Tap Existing Data to Profile Community Health Status," *The Quality Letter,* vol. 10, no. 1, January 1998, pp. 17–18. ARTICLE.

Trustee Education

Bader, Barry S. "Ten Pathways to High-Performance Boards in Integrated Health Systems," *Health System Leader*, vol. 4, no. 10, November 1997, pp. 4–11. ARTICLE.

Holland, Thomas P., Roger A. Ritvo, and Anthony R. Kovner. *Improving Board Effectiveness: Practical Lessons for Nonprofit Health Care Organizations* (Chicago: American Hospital Publishing, Inc., 1997). [ISBN 1-55648-181-0]. BOOK.

Kovner, Anthony R. "Board Development in Two Hospitals: Lessons from a Demonstration," *Hospital and Health Services Administration,* vol. 42, no. 1, Spring 1997, pp. 87–99. ARTICLE.

Orlikoff, James E., and Mary K. Totten. *The Trustee Handbook for Health Care Governance* (Chicago: American Hospital Publishing, Inc., 1998). [ISBN 1-55648-220-5]. (Compilation of four trustee guides: *The Trustee Guide to Boardroom Basics in Health Care, The Trustee Guide to Board Accountability in Health Care, The Trustee Guide to Strategic Planning and Information in Health Care,* and *The Trustee Guide to Board Relations in Health Care.*) BOOK.

Liability Issues

Burdett, Robert J., Jr. *Director Liability: A Guide to Preventing Trouble in the Hospital Boardroom* (Chicago: American Hospital Publishing, Inc., 1991). [ISBN 1-55648-067-9]. BOOK.

Shinkman, Ron. "Consolidation Trend Increases Odds for Conflicts of Interest," *Modern Healthcare,* vol. 28, no. 3, January 19, 1998, pp. 30, 32. ARTICLE.

Wachel, Walter. "When in Doubt, Deal Yourself Out," *Healthcare Executive,* vol. 8, no. 5, September-October 1993, pp. 4–7. ARTICLE.

Duty to Care/Loyalty

Beckham, J. Daniel. "The Accountability Crisis in Healthcare," *Healthcare Forum Journal,* vol. 40, no. 5, September-October 1997, pp. 34–37. ARTICLE.

N.J.S.A. 15A:6-14. (New Jersey Statutes Annotated Title 15A: Corporations, Nonprofit, Chapter 6–14 "Standard of Care . . ."). LAW.

Principles and Guidelines for Changes in Hospital Ownership (Chicago: American Hospital Publishing, Inc., 1997). BROCHURE.

Smith, D. H. *Entrusted: The Moral Responsibilities of Trusteeship* (Bloomington, IN: Indiana University Press, 1995). BOOK.

Board Responsibilities

While individual trustees bear specific personal responsibilities, entire boards bear major collective responsibilities. Examples include: fulfilling the organization's mission, fiduciary oversight, ensuring solid executive performance, engaging in broad policy approval and strategic planning, and program oversight.

Fulfilling the Mission

The most important work of any governing board is to create and, as appropriate, recreate the reason for organizational existence. Therefore, the first question any effective board should ask is: "What is the mission and vision of my organization?" The answer should be put on paper—in the form of a mission statement. But it doesn't end there.

Any board—given the time—can write a powerful mission statement. But its true power lies in usage. If the statement merely finds a quiet resting place in grant applications, annual reports, and brochures, it is useless and a waste of the board's time. It is up to the board to ensure not only that an appropriate and succinct mission is crafted, but also that it is lived daily.

No one contends this is an easy thing to do. Ian Morrison, a noted management consultant and senior fellow at the Institute for the Future in Menlo Park, California, once told an audience of health care leaders of a blunder he'd made in advising Volvo on an

37

emerging market. Morrison suggested that the auto maker build a minivan or, better yet, a sports utility vehicle to remain competitive. Without hesitation, the CEO told Morrison that Volvo would never make a minivan or sports utility vehicle because it was not possible to make a safe one. "End of story," said Morrison. "Volvo walked away from billions of dollars because its values were real. Its mission was safety. Health systems must look at their values and mission statement, see if they're real, and then behave as if they matter."

Fiduciary Oversight

In fulfilling the mission of their organization, trustees are faced with the delicate balance of ensuring that the financial resources necessary to implement needed programs and services are available and in place while protecting the organization's financial status.

POINTS TO PONDER

➤ When was the last time you revisited your organization's mission statement? How do you, personally, live out the mission of your organization?

➤ Do you understand your organization's financial statements and issues? How do you obtain clarification of issues you don't understand?

➤ What type of relationship do you have with your CEO? Do you view the board-CEO relationship as a partnership or simply as an employer-employee relationship?

➤ How is the CEO made aware of the board's goals and parameters for operations?

In managing assets, trustees have three primary fiduciary duties: obedience, care, and loyalty. Obedience requires board members to obey the law, make sure the hospital/health system obeys the law, and carry out the hospital's mission and bylaws. Care requires that board members are prudent in managing the organization's financial affairs. Loyalty requires governing board members always to put the hospital's or health system's interests ahead of the personal interests of business, associates, friends, and relatives.

While boards are accountable for budgets, the budget document itself should not be their focus. Rather, what good is done for people—and at what cost—is what board members should keep in mind. As governance expert John Carver notes: "Fiduciary responsibility does not mean controlling the number of phone lines, but it does mean controlling the ability to pay the bills. It does not mean controlling

CASES IN POINT

Mission: "In the late 1980s, the board of Chisago Health (now part of Fairview Health System) in Forest Lake, Minnesota, revamped its mission statement to take a more proactive stance toward improving the health of its community. Part of the vision was to start with the core roots of the community— children and families. A partnership composed of health leaders, educators, business executives, and law enforcement and government officials was formed. Taking an assets-based approach to strengthening families, Families First! was launched with just $3,500 from the Fairview Foundation. "It's extremely rewarding to recognize the difference this partnership is making in the community and in individual families," says CEO Scott Wordelman, "which is what we're all about."

(Excerpted from *Trustee,* vol. 50, no. 7, July/August 1997, by permission. Copyright 1997, American Hospital Publishing, Inc.).

Board-CEO Relationships: Gordon Sprenger, CEO of Allina Healthcare System, Minneapolis, reports: "For years my board judged me on [hospital] occupancy. If we went below 80 percent, they wanted to know why more patients weren't coming to the hospital. Now, in moving from a patient model to a member model, we look at the number of lives we're responsible for—those looking to Allina to manage their health status. This is a major paradigm shift."

out-of-state travel, but it does mean controlling the conservatism with which revenues are projected."

Although boards are responsible for financial operations, board members themselves do not need to be financial experts. Instead, they should consult credentialed experts—CPAs, major auditing firms—to ensure that the organization is in compliance with legal and regulatory mandates. They should also require a management letter from the auditor detailing processes that need examination and improvement, and ensure that safeguards are in place, such as an effective corporate compliance program.

Understanding—being able to read and interpret—financial statements is critical. Carver notes: "Boards put great stock in monthly or quarterly financial reports. Yet a substantial number of board members do not understand these reports. Even in boards composed of persons competent at analyzing financial statements, it is uncommon for the board to know—as a body—what it finds acceptable."

Many boards use financial and auditing committees composed of members well versed in financial/analytical issues who report back to the larger board. The bottom line is, however, that all board members—regardless of the existence or nonexistence of a financial or auditing committee—must understand financial issues and statements. They must be prepared to intelligently discuss financial issues and ask questions about anything they don't understand. And they must take the initiative to request that financial information is presented in an easy-to-read, easy-to-understand manner.

The Board-CEO Relationship

Although the board both finds and hires the CEO, a military, hierarchical relationship should not exist between the board and CEO. A critical point often misunderstood—and sometimes just never known by trustees—is that individual trustees and CEOs are colleagues and equals. And that includes the board chair as well.

"When trustees amass as a group and form the board, the CEO reports to the board, but that doesn't mean that every trustee has some kind of legal right to lord it over the CEO," says Keith Pryor, himself a former hospital CEO. "The CEO reports to the board collectively, but does not report to individual trustees."

BOARD JOB DESCRIPTIONS

Job descriptions are increasingly being used to help board members better understand their roles and responsibilities. Specifically, job descriptions serve several important purposes, including:

➤ *New board recruitment:* Allows candidates to know precisely what is expected of them should they join the board

➤ *Board self-evaluation:* Provides a foundation for evaluating board performance

➤ *Keeping governance on track:* Points out when the board is drifting away from performing key roles and responsibilities and enables fine-tuning on a regular basis

➤ *Preventing conflict among multiple boards:* Clarifies which board has authority to do what

➤ *Distinguishing between governance and management:* Helps both sides understand and respect the limits of each other's responsibilities

(Adapted from James Orlikoff, "Trustee Workbook," *Trustee,* vol. 50, no. 1, January 1997, by permission. Copyright 1997, American Hospital Publishing, Inc. The following sample board job description first appeared in this article.)

"The board provides oversight for programmatic and policy-related aspects of all hospital services and corporate activities consistent with the Articles of Incorporation. Appoints the CEO and approves all actions of the Executive Committee taken in the name of the board between meetings.

"Further, the board adopts and adheres to statements of mission, vision, strategy and values that are reviewed on a regular basis. Considers the health requirements of the community and how the hospital can meet them. Determines the scope of programs and services and the desired levels of quality. Provides advice and counsel to the CEO in the implementation of plans and programs."

Written job descriptions should be made available to the entire board delineating the roles, responsibilities, and expectations of trustees, the board chair, and the CEO. With the reporting relationship clearly defined, trustees and CEOs can then begin working together toward common goals. One of those goals is making the CEO's job more doable by placing it within a strategic framework and establishing the parameters for operations to achieve the board's mission using prioritized goals. As stated earlier, the organization's mission should be the foundation upon which all strategic decisions are based, particularly the guidance given to the CEO.

The board should measure the CEO's performance against strategic goals. "You can't do it all," says Andre Delbecq, professor of business and administration at Santa Clara University, in the February 1997 issue of *Trustee* magazine. "You can't be an academic medical center that is focused on furthering basic scientific knowledge and a community-owned hospital focused on wellness and a tertiary care center. You have to say, 'Here is who we are. This is what makes sense in our community and our competitive environment, and we are going to manage according to that focus.'" By periodically examining how well the organization is progressing in its strategic direction, a board of trustees lets its CEO know whether or not he or she is on the right track so that corrective measures can be undertaken in a timely manner.

POINTS TO PONDER

➤ Do you view the big picture in terms of policy? Or do you allow yourself to become bogged down in detail? How much time do you spend creating the future (planning, setting policy, making decisions) versus monitoring the past?

➤ Does your board routinely assess its performance? How do you, as an individual trustee, assess your talents and contributions to the organization?

But perhaps most important is that the board concentrate on fulfilling its own responsibilities, allow the CEO to do his or her own job, and understand that it has no official connection with staff members except at the CEO's behest. That means supporting the CEO as a staff leader and as a human being, not undercutting his or her decisions, speaking to various factions in a single voice, and, above all, reaffirming the mission of the institution. It is well to understand that the CEO's performance cannot be judged fairly without the board assessing how well *it* did in guiding and providing feedback to the CEO.

Policy Approval and Agenda Control

An easy rule of thumb for any board, according to Pryor, is "that if something crosses the board table that seems to be too detailed—it probably is."

Trustees must be careful not to become bogged down in the minu-tiae of policy development. Instead, they should take a more Supreme Court-like stance: listen to proposals made by executives and physicians, weigh the pros and cons in terms of the organization's overall mission, and cast the final nay or

---

CASE IN POINT

Self-Evaluation: During the summer of 1996, the New Jersey Hospital Association surveyed board chairs of member hospitals to determine their current self-evaluation practices. Responses indicated that all but two of the boards evaluated performance annually. The most common form of evaluation was for each board member to evaluate the board as a whole. Many boards used combined methods, including evaluation of individual performance, written evaluation, group discussion, and oral evaluation. Areas reviewed were consistent and included: board and individual board member effectiveness; planning; and financial, quality, management, and community oversight. Boards also examined other areas significant to their own hospital mission and operations such as marketing; system relationships; oversight of fund-raising, investment, and risk management; mission and culture; and employee relations. Most often, the boards incorporated the results of their self-evaluation into quality improvement plans or used the results to identify educational needs.

yea. "Making staff decisions trivializes the board's job, disempowers staff, interferes with staff investment, and reduces the degree to which the CEO can be accountable for outcomes," says Carver.

In looking to the future, boards must control the board room agenda so that discussions focus on planning, setting policy, and making forward-thinking decisions. "When times were relatively stable and prosperous, a typical board spent most of its time monitoring the past," says governance expert James Orlikoff. "The information the board received and its agenda were largely devoted to reviews of what happened last month, last quarter, or last year." Today, Orlikoff says that talking about the past (monitoring) should be reduced to no more than 25 percent of a board's time and talking about—and creating—the future should consume the other 75 percent.

Board Self-Evaluation

A board has a responsibility to monitor its own performance both as a collective body and as individual trustees. "One of the most reliable ways the board of a nonprofit organization can strengthen its performance as a governing body is to assess periodically its own performance," writes Larry H. Slesinger in *Self-Assessment for Non-Profit Governing Boards.*

Board self-evaluations should be conducted for three key reasons: The current environment demands excellence in governance, effective evaluation can improve performance, and self-evaluations satisfy the Joint Commission on Accreditation of Healthcare Organizations standard that "leaders must measure and assess the effectiveness of their contributions to performance improvement." Specifically, the process should answer the following questions:

- What are we doing well?
- Did we meet our objectives?
- What areas need improvement?
- How can we make the necessary changes?
- How can the improvements be sustained?

RECOMMENDED READING

BOARD RESPONSIBILITIES

"Mission: Do the Right Thing When It Comes to Your Community; Do You Know What That Is?" *Trustee,* vol. 50, no. 5, May 1997, pp. 16–21. ARTICLE.

Mission and the Marketplace: Striking the Balance (Audiocassette), HRET/Trustee Institute Audio Series (Princeton: Health Research and Educational Trust of New Jersey, 1997). AUDIOCASSETTE.

Orlikoff, James. E. "Trouble in the Boardroom: The Seven Deadly Sins of Ineffective Governance," *Healthcare Forum Journal,* vol. 40, no. 4, July-August 1997, pp. 38–42. ARTICLE.

A Guide to Self-Evaluation for Hospital Governing Boards (Princeton: New Jersey Hospital Association, Council on Hospital Governance, 1996).

Board/CEO Relationships

Bader, Barry S. "Board/CEO Relationship Builders" (five-part series), in *Hospitals & Health Networks,* 1997. ($35.00 in lots of 10; to order, call 800-AHA-2626). ARTICLES.

Greene, Jan. "How Does Your CEO Spell 'Relief'?" *Trustee,* vol. 51, no. 8, September 1997, pp. 9–14. ARTICLE.

"Leadership," in *1998 Hospital Accreditation Standards* (Chicago: Joint Commission on Accreditation of Healthcare Organizations, 1998), pp. 139–58. [ISBN 0-86688-575-7]. BOOK CHAPTER.

"Management," in *1998 Hospital Accreditation Standards* (Chicago: Joint Commission on Accreditation of Healthcare Organizations, 1998), pp. 221–24. [ISBN 0-86688-575-7]. BOOK CHAPTER.

Sandrick, K. M. "How to Support Your CEO: In a Stress-Filled World, the Board Can Be the CEO's Worst Nightmare or a Dream Come True," *Trustee,* vol. 50, no. 2, February 1997, pp. 14–18. ARTICLE.

Board and Committee Structures

As the health care industry has changed and evolved, one of the major consequences is that there are fewer stand-alone hospitals and, subsequently, fewer stand-alone hospital boards. With the consolidation and merging of individual hospitals have come new board structures and committees. While local hospital boards remain important, there are now health care system boards, regional boards, advisory boards, and foundation boards. According to governance expert Keith Pryor, it is important for trustees to understand the roles and responsibilities of each.

"The type of work being done at the system level may not necessarily appeal to an individual who wants to feel closely connected to an individual hospital or community," says Pryor. "It's important that trustees—both seasoned and new—understand the difference."

Generally speaking, system boards see the strategic plan as their primary document, while local boards are more engaged with community concerns and institution specifics.

Gerald McManis, president and CEO of McManis Association, a health care consulting firm based in Washington, D.C., is just one of many futurists predicting a consolidation of board structures. "Ultimately, local boards will have community orientation rather than fiduciary responsibility," he says. "They'll be responsible for asking whether community needs are being met, they'll work with community groups, but they'll have less to do with resource allocation. System boards will have a much higher level of responsibility and will include more health care industry experts than community representatives. They are also likely to be paid."

Of course, there are other types of boards as well. Regional boards are on the rise as systems form and increasingly cut across large geographic regions. As with system boards, visioning and strategic planning are their major emphasis. Foundation boards charged with raising funds continue to provide needed additional financial support for their hospital or health system.

As not-for-profit hospitals are sold to for-profit entities, charitable foundations or trusts have been

POINTS TO PONDER

➤ How do you differentiate the role of the health system board versus local hospital board or foundation board?

➤ What is your role and what is expected of the board on which you serve?

➤ What vision does your organization have for future board structure? How are you moving in that direction?

➤ Are physicians represented at your board table? How has increased physician representation influenced the work and direction of your board?

➤ If you are a member of a board committee, are you familiar with the committee's specific charge? Do you understand your role? Have you determined whether a long-standing or short-term committee is best suited to carry out that charge?

➤ As you assist in identifying future members to serve on your board, what competencies and skill sets are most critical?

created. The monies from the sale of institutions are returned to the community through the foundation or trust and managed by a board. *Trustee* magazine reports that as of September 1997, 81 foundations have been created through "conversions" from not-for-profit to for-profit status.

"Foundation governance differs from hospital governance in its more ongoing hands-on approach—not only in determining mission and gauging the health status of the community, but also in tracking how funding is maintained," says David Zacharias, president of the Foundation Advisory in Phoenix, Arizona.

The proper size of a board depends on its roles and responsibilities. Typically, however, integrated system boards should be smaller, focusing on big-picture strategy issues, while local boards may be larger, more representative of the community, and focused on quality of care, credentialing, and community-based issues.

"There's no one right answer when it comes to health care governance size," says Edward McGrath in the January 1998 issue of *Trustee* magazine. "But in most cases, downsizing a board to between 10 and 20 members is the right thing to do. Smaller boards tend to attract talented, energetic leaders who welcome the ability to have more input and don't like to be just another face lost in the crowd."

There also appears to be no magic-bullet formula for the number of boards that should be employed within a system or how power should ultimately be distributed. Some systems are electing to diminish the power of local boards and centralizing all decision making at the corporate level. Others are leaving their local boards intact even if it leads to more complex governance. Henry Ford Health System in Detroit, for example, currently has 8 hospitals, 70 ambulatory care centers, 2 nursing homes, 50 optical shops, and a health plan. Each has its own board—amounting to about 300 trustees.

Many organizations are resting somewhere in between a streamlined and a complex governance structure.

Futurist Russell C. Coile Jr. adds that health system board members may have to be credentialed. "Physicians must be credentialed before they can be appointed and reappointed to a medical staff, managed care panel, or physician-hospital organization. Why not trustees?" One such criterion could be past governance experience. At least one health system—Sutter Health in California—may be moving toward implementation of board credentialing.

BOARD CHAIRS SPEAK OUT ON MERGERS AND FUTURE BOARD STRUCTURES

In 1995, the executive search firm Spencer Stuart and *Trustee* magazine surveyed 500 board chairs of medium-sized hospitals. Of those responding, 89 percent agreed that most hospitals will merge with another hospital or system during the next five years. But many had serious concerns about a merger.

Half said they were concerned about losing their mission, identity, and/or focus and giving up control. Twenty percent worried about conflicting corporate cultures after a merger. And 30 percent feared selecting the wrong partner or that the merger wouldn't be worth the costs involved.

When it came to predicting how their current hospital boards would pan out, the majority tended to agree that new system boards would bear the bulk of the strategic and fiduciary responsibility. Half saw the new boards as "being more broad-minded and professional." The remainder feared that system boards would be less concerned about local issues and more concerned with the bottom line.

As for those serving on the local level, respondents described the ideal future trustee as being committed to mission and the community, business oriented, and knowledgeable about the health care industry.

Physician Representation and New Board Structures

In recent years there has been movement to place more physicians on hospital boards. "Physicians certainly have a major stake in health care delivery and not to give them a major voice at the policy-making table is to say, 'We don't think you're that important'," says Dick Shive, trustee at Somerset Medical Center in New Jersey, in the January 1998 issue of *Trustee* magazine.

Until recently the Internal Revenue Service limited "interested parties"—which included doctors—to 20 percent representation on not-for-profit boards. But under revised IRS guidelines, such boards can have more than 20 percent representation by interested parties provided that a conflict-of-interest policy is in place. For example, physicians must refrain from participating in decisions in which they have an economic interest.

But hospital boards are not the only place in which physicians are gaining leadership positions. The emergence of physician-hospital organizations and management

---

CASES IN POINT

Board Structures: Sutter Health in California is taking a streamlined approach with the governance of its eight hospitals, six long-term care facilities, and seven medical groups. According to Elaine Donaldson, board chairman for Sutter Roseville Medical Center, Sutter is currently consolidating its seven local boards into one regional board. The local groups will then convert to advisory committees that represent community concerns. The reason? "It's difficult to make timely decisions when executives have to go through several levels of board approval," says Donaldson. Sutter's parent board comprises only a handful of members—all well versed in health care. Included are a retired doctor, academic nurse, health care economist, retired legislator, and venture capitalist. All are paid.

Committee Structures: When Greater Southeast Community Healthcare System in Washington, D.C., initiated a task force to examine the board's purpose and structure, it identified a set of critical questions for members to ask themselves. "Answering those questions led us to recommend that we remove from our bylaws the requirement that we have standing committees," says trustee Carolyn B. Lewis, also a member of the American Hospital Association's board of directors. "Although this sounds like a simple sort of administrative decision, it really freed up our thinking to understand that we needed to have the board form committees that would accomplish the board's unique work and not mirror staff's work. For example, we are now forming a committee that will look at integration—a committee that will affiliate, in an informal way, with other boards around town to talk about what is going on in their systems. Our board is very excited with the idea that we will be doing committee work that directly ties into the board's work plan."

service organizations has actually pulled physicians and hospitals closer together—resulting in brand new board structures. On many of these boards, physicians hold as many as 50 percent of the seats.

Committee Structures

As board structures change, it is only natural for traditional board committee structures to also give way. In the past, long-standing board committees have included personnel, executive, program, finance, and nomination.

But according to John Carver, there are no "right" committees— no list of correct subdivisions for getting a job done. "None of the common committees is indispensable; there is no one committee a board must have," he says. Governance consultant James Orlikoff notes that long-standing committees can sometimes hinder board productivity, particularly when it comes to setting the board agenda.

"Most board agendas don't change over time," says Orlikoff. "Too often the agenda gets set in stone. If you have standing committees that never change, you're always going to have standing committee reports which will take up to 50 percent of your agenda. The static nature of board agendas is one of the single biggest problems I see throughout governance. Part of the problem is that we as trustees like that: The agenda packet always looks the same so we know when we can pay attention and when we don't need to pay attention. And that is what lulls boards into a false sense of security."

RECOMMENDED READING

BOARD AND COMMITTEE STRUCTURES

American Hospital Association and Ernst & Young, LLP. *Shining Light on Your Board's Passage to the Future* (Chicago: American Hospital Association and Ernst & Young, 1997). BOOK.

Orlikoff, James E., and Mary K. Totten. "Community Representation and the Effective Board," *Trustee,* vol. 51, no. 1, January 1998, suppl.; 4 pp. ARTICLE.

Orlikoff, James E., and Mary K. Totten. *The Future of Health Care Governance: Redesigning Boards for a New Era* (Chicago: American Hospital Publishing, Inc., 1996). [ISBN 1-55648-160-8]. BOOK.

Role and Functions of the Hospital Governing Board, Management Advisory Series (Chicago: American Hospital Publishing, Inc., 1990), 5 pp. BROCHURE.

Savage, Grant T., Rosemary L. Taylor, Timothy M. Rotarius, and John A. Buesseler. "Governance of Integrated Delivery Systems/Networks: A Stakeholder Approach," *Health Care Management Review,* vol. 22, no. 1, Winter 1997, pp. 7–20. ARTICLE.

Board Operations

When it comes to the actual shirt-sleeve-rolled, hard-core work of the hospital and health system board, it all comes down to meetings. The board's authority to act is derived from its being in session as a collective body with the presence of a quorum. Clearly, this makes board members' limited time together a very precious commodity that requires efficiency and effectiveness in the way they carry out their work.

Trustees have a responsibility to attend meetings regularly, to prepare in advance by reading the agenda and background materials, and, most important, to participate, listen, question, and debate. Otherwise they're not doing their jobs.

On any given day in hospital and health system boardrooms throughout the country, six issues are on the agenda: strategic planning, executive performance, financial oversight, community accountability, quality of care, and advocacy.

In some boardrooms, individual committees are addressing these issues. Other boards, having dissolved long-standing committees, are addressing the issues more collectively or initiating issue-oriented committees associated with strategic goal areas. Many are somewhere in between. Regardless of how work is being carried out, it is imperative for all board members to be up-to-date on the key responsibilities entrusted to them and to willingly accept leadership posts.

POINTS TO PONDER

➤ How does your strategic plan account for and respond to environmental/marketplace change and the evolving needs of your institution and community?

➤ How does your organization's financial plan/ status complement its strategic plan?

➤ How does your board establish and maintain open and supportive dialogue with the CEO on goals and performance?

Strategic Planning

Developing and maintaining a meaningful mission statement and long-range strategic plan are fundamental governing board responsibilities. Defining the hospital or health system's reason for being, its vision for the future, and recommended course of action to fulfill that vision are among the most important contributions a board can make to the effectiveness of the organization. (See *Board Responsibilities,* p. 37.)

"If the board is clear about what it wants to accomplish and how it's going to do that, it can then interpret and translate its mission and vision to help steer it toward the direction it wants to go,"

says trustee Carolyn B. Lewis. "Management can then put a plan together that fits within that framework. It's an interactive process."

The mission statement defines what the organization is and why it exists. It is the cornerstone of the strategic plan and drives the course of action the hospital or health system will adopt to achieve its goals and objectives. Many boards write mission statements several paragraphs or even pages long, but, according to author John Carver, mission statements can be stated in just a few carefully chosen words—with several more detailed policy statements added. Even more important than the succinctness of the mission statement, however, is that the mission be lived daily. "Trustees must keep the dream out in front so members always see the relationship of mundane things like budgets and audits in the context of the 'glorious outcomes' that they have come together to achieve," says Carver.

Ultimately, with mission and vision clearly defined, a recommended course of action (strategic plan) can be enacted to fulfill that vision. Strategic planning is the process of determining what an organization wants to be in the future and how it will get there.

CASES IN POINT

Strategic Planning: The reevaluation of mission statements has resulted in some very innovative and distinctive outreach. Following is a sample highlighted in New York State Hospitals' *Vital Community Resources,* a joint publication of the Hospital Association of New York State and the Hospital Trustees of New York State: The medical center "has no reason being on its own; it exists only to serve the needs of its neighbors. [The medical center] defines health as the total well-being of the community and its residents. Beyond the absence of individual physical illness, this includes, at least, decent housing, the ability to speak English, employment and educational opportunities, and civic participation. . . ."

Executive Performance: When outside auditors reviewed Advocate Health Care's executive compensation program, only one thing was lacking: the attendant concern and anguish that frequently accompanies such reviews. The high marks the program received came as no surprise to board members. After all, since Advocate's creation, the board had been intimately involved in the development of an effective, performance-driven executive pay strategy. "If you look at the millions we spend on salaries, we ought to pay a lot of attention to it," says Robert G. McLennan, who chairs the board and its compensation committee. The process also offers liability protection for board members. Under tough new Internal Revenue Service rules on excessive pay, trustees can find themselves personally liable if the organizations they govern are found to be overcompensating not only executives, but also physicians.

(Adapted from *Trustee,* vol. 51, no. 6, June 1997, by permission. Copyright 1997, American Hospital Publishing, Inc.)

Strategic planning is different from short-term or operational planning. Strategic planning requires choices about the hospital's or health system's future. To be effective, meaningful, and relevant, the strategic plan needs to be viewed as a dynamic, "living" document. Some boards spend many months and thousands of dollars developing a plan report that thereafter they only consult and review annually—and find that it has become outdated and less useful. To remain vital and meaningful, the strategic plan must account for and respond to environmental change in the marketplace and community, prepare for the evolving needs of the hospital or health system to meet changing demands, limit risks, and allocate limited resources most constructively on priority strategies.

Executive Performance

No single relationship in the organization is as important as that between the board and its chief executive officer. (See *Board Responsibilities,* p. 37.) Although board members and CEOs are viewed as colleagues, trustees play a major role in CEO selection and performance evaluation.

In terms of executive performance, it should never come as a surprise to the CEO that the board is satisfied—or dissatisfied. The board and CEO should have in place an agreed-upon evaluation process spelling out what both expect to accomplish in the coming year. The American Hospital Association reports that 81 percent of health care systems have implemented formal CEO performance evaluations. In some instances, the trend is to link CEO performance goals with compensation dollars.

The CEO performance evaluation is sensitive for various reasons. Jordan Hadelman, president and CEO of national health care executive search firm Witt/Kieffer, Ford, Hadelman and Lloyd, notes that trustees are often embarrassed about criticizing the CEO, who may also be their friend or golf partner, while CEOs may believe that the board has no true grasp of health issues and is looking only at the bottom line. Each may be waiting for the other to make the first move. But in such cases, Hadelman contends that trustees are ultimately responsible.

"CEO evaluation is the board's most serious duty—an obligation that can't be shirked or endlessly postponed until the roof falls in," he says. "It's why trustees are on the board—to provide the professional executive with guidance on the organization's mission and to reward success when it is achieved." Following are tips to make the process smoother:

- Involve the CEO in every stage of the process.

- Hire a consultant to facilitate and conduct salary/benefit surveys.
- Establish and maintain real dialogue with the CEO on goals and rewards.
- Listen to the CEO's opinions.
- Agree on goals and regularly keep tabs at predetermined times throughout the year.
- Review the process at year-end, reward accomplishments, and set new goals and rewards for the coming year.

Fiduciary Oversight

The hospital or health system governing board is accountable to its owners. But this charge differs greatly from commercial enterprises. In the corporate culture, boards are accountable to clearly defined owners—their investors. They judge success by straightforward measures, principally profitability and growth in equity. Customer satisfaction and quality are means, but not ends in themselves. In addition, public companies can choose the markets they serve. They are not required to serve those who can't pay or offer products that are needed but lose money.

That does not mean that not-for-profit organizations should not have a surplus of monies. In fact, a surplus is necessary for boards to provide the financial resources necessary to meet future needs.

It is important for boards to understand the financial implications of an organization's strategic plan. The challenge is to be willing to accept risk, to weigh the consequences intelligently, and to maximize the impact of any failures on the organization. It is also important for board members to understand that they are accountable to multiple entities and that goals such as improved community health and enhanced access for the poor are very difficult to measure.

Barry Bader, a prominent governance consultant, offers this analogy: "A retail chain stays open 24 hours a day only if extended hours generate profits," he says. "By contrast, many community-owned hospitals lose money keeping ERs open all night or maintaining clinics in low-income areas. Both public company and hospital boards must ensure financial viability, but the company board jeopardizes its fiduciary responsibility if it OKs activities that reduce shareholder value. By contrast, the hospital and health system board services its fiduciary role

CASE IN POINT

Community Accountability: In Atlantic City, New Jersey, not far from the high-rise glitz and glamour of the city's casinos, a group of residents, city officials, business owners, religious leaders, health care providers, and educators gather. They are clad in uniform white "Up With Hope, Down with Dope" T-shirts and hard hats. They are committed to taking back their streets and residential neighborhoods from the drug deals that hold many citizens hostage in their own homes.

"We're fired up," says Russ Patterson, a cocktail waitress from the city's tough Chelsea neighborhood. "We're out here tonight to show there is zero tolerance in Atlantic City for drug dealing. No one is going to stand on my corner or in my neighborhood and sell genocide. We're taking back our streets."

AtlantiCare Health System invested more than $150,000 to launch the Turn Around Atlantic City program and orchestrated the marches, which will continue weekly for a minimum of three years in what leaders call a "weeding" (driving known drug dealers out of town) and "seeding" (introducing opportunities for employment, education, and quality of life) process. A community health assessment survey, initiated by AtlantiCare in 1996, flagged drugs as the city's number one community—and health—concern.

"Last year, 253 babies were admitted to Atlantic City Medical Center's neonatal intensive care unit, and of those babies, 75 percent were born with drugs already in their system. You can see that drugs are quite a crisis for this community, so that investing in this [Turn Around Atlantic City] is money well spent," says Dorothea Metzler, chairman of the board of governors for the medical center.

(Excerpted from *Trustee,* March 1998, with permission. Copyright 1998, American Hospital Publishing, Inc.)

by both meeting community needs and not going broke."

Ultimately, the board is accountable for the oversight of hospital or system finances and other operations. Only the board can strike the balance needed on questions of values and ethics: Shall we maintain certain needed community services even if they are unprofitable? To what extent can we provide services to those who cannot afford to pay for their care? To what extent will we collaborate with our neighboring hospitals and physicians, and to what extent must we compete? What kind of ownership—public, private, not-for-profit, or for-profit—will best assure the institution's future?

The survival and success of the organization depend on skillful and careful management of the hospital's assets. Most boards and finance committees are well equipped for this function, including among their members bankers, business owners, attorneys, and others experienced in financial management. They have the ability to perform such board functions as review and approval of the operating and capital budgets, proposals for new services, and plans for new equipment acquisition. The challenge for the board is to distinguish between boardsmanship and meddling in operations, between active oversight and simply rubber-stamping.

Community Accountability

Community accountability is, in many ways, the crux of what hospital and health system trusteeism is all about. "Hospitals exist to serve their communities," says Carolyn B. Lewis. "They are accountable to the public for spending resources prudently and in the community's best interest. If the board does not resemble the community, then the community and the institution are at risk. Simply put, we don't see things as they are; we see them as we are."

Ensuring community accountability goes way beyond securing community representation on the board, however. Most important, it involves getting in touch—at a grassroots level—with the needs of the communities.

In more and more states—California, New York, Texas, Utah—hospitals are now required by law to demonstrate accountability to their community. They must do so by conducting community-based needs assessments to identify unmet needs, partner with other health providers and community-based agencies, and implement programs to meet those needs in measurable ways that can be communicated to the community. It is important to note, of course, that many hospitals in states not required by law to demonstrate community accountability—including New Jersey—are in fact doing so. Because it's the right thing to do.

To be truly accountable, hospitals and health systems must redefine their community and take responsibility for the community's overall health and well-being. They must work with others in the community as good corporate neighbors to combat the issues affecting quality of life such as teen pregnancies, drugs, and violence.

Quality of Care

Quality has never been easy to define, particularly in the health care arena. As the focus of health care shifts from inpatients and sickness to community-based prevention and wellness, it will only become harder still to define. Health care boards bear ultimate responsibility for the quality of patient care provided in and by their institutions.

How does a governing board fulfill its responsibilities for assuring the quality of patient care? In several ways, namely: creating a relationship of mutual trust and respect with physicians, medical staff credentialing, and total quality improvement (TQI). Following is a look at each.

Medical Staff Relationships

Much of the authority for delivering high-quality care rests with the medical staff, but that does not mean that the board is not responsible as well. Ultimate accountability for ensuring high-quality care rests with the board. It is imperative, therefore, that the board, CEO, and medical staff share a feeling of mutual trust and respect. And it is up to the board to forge this relationship—to make sure that physicians have

meaningful participation, not only in the policy-making process, but in planning and finance as well.

In progressive organizations throughout the country, physicians are increasingly in board-appointed leadership positions. Mike Turner, president and CEO of Somerset Medical Center in Somerville, New Jersey, comments: "Nobody understands the operation of a hospital better than its customers, and physicians are key customers. They're here at all hours and they see how the organization responds to their needs and to the needs of patients. As the board wrestles with the issue of how to become more cost effective, there's tremendous value in having physicians at the table as fellow stakeholders and having them work as liaisons with colleagues."

Medical Staff Credentialing

One of the most important tasks of health care governance boards is medical staff credentialing. Many trustees find the credentialing process intimidating because it has significant implications for physicians, the hospital, and the community at large. The object of credentialing is to ensure that only qualified doctors are admitted (and remain on) a hospital's medical staff and that they practice within their scope of experience and competence.

According to governance consultant Dennis Pointer, boards have two roles to play in physician credentialing. First, they must oversee the process, making sure it is fair, consistent, and functioning effectively. Second, board members must decide on which doctors will be admitted to the hospital's medical staff (appointment) and which will be allowed to remain (reappointment).

"Although the medical staff forwards recommendations, board members must make the final decisions," says Pointer. "Boards must make these decisions independently; that is, members cannot merely rubber-stamp credentialing recommendations that have been forwarded by the medical staff. Although trustees are not expected to be expert on all the laws and regulations governing the credentialing process, they are expected to be informed. I recommend that an in-service educational program on credentialing be conducted for the board every several years."

Total Quality Improvement

In looking at the big picture on quality initiatives, progressive organizations are increasingly looking beyond quality assurance programs (the meeting of standards by the Joint Commission on Accreditation of Healthcare Organizations [JCAHO], Departments of Health, and other licensing agencies) to improve the processes and systems in place to ensure quality beyond traditional clinical definitions. TQI focuses on making an entire system's outcomes better by constantly adjusting and improving the system itself, as opposed to searching out and getting rid of the "bad apples." It must motivate every worker, from dietary staff to physicians and senior management. Again, board members must be careful not to become bogged down in details, but instead must encourage the vision and provide the resources for a more efficient, more patient-focused quality environment. In New Jersey, for example, Saint Barnabas Health Care System has instituted patient satisfaction departments at each of its nine affiliate hospitals. Patient satisfaction has reportedly soared at each facility.

CASES IN POINT

Medical Staff Credentialing: According to Kevin Wardell, executive vice president of Advocate Health Care, "The biggest single accountability of the governing councils is medical staff credentialing, and that is new. In the Evangelical Health System (now part of Advocate), credentialing decisions were passed from the councils to the system board. We've passed the accountability back down for a couple of reasons: One is the sheer impracticality of having a single body make credible decisions about some 3,500 physicians; the other is to make it more satisfying for council members to participate so that we can continue to recruit and retain excellent people."

Total Quality Improvement: For months, board members and executive staff at Griffin Hospital in Derby, Connecticut, labored to hammer out a vision for the hospital, which ultimately was to create a more holistic environment for patients and family members. The mission was initiated after five members of Griffin's leadership, within an 18-month period, became patients on the receiving end of health care delivery. "In walking away from those experiences none of us were enthralled with the hospital delivery system as it existed in and outside Connecticut," says William Powanda, a Griffin vice president.

The experiment in changing patient care began in labor and delivery. Women of child-bearing age were asked what they would want in a childbirth center. For more than a year, women were surveyed—women who had children, who didn't have children, who had delivered at Griffin, who chose not to

JCAHO

Since 1980, the JCAHO has required a problem-oriented approach to quality assurance. The hospital, its physicians, and other providers of care must monitor critical indicators of patient care—like death, infections, adverse occurrences—and must identify problems and potential problems.

The JCAHO also has specific requirements regarding the leadership of health care organizations; specifically, that leaders regularly assess community needs, review the hospital's mission, adjust the hospital's plan for services to meet newly identified needs, and support principles and methods of continuous

---

CASES IN POINT (Continued)

deliver at Griffin. After seemingly endless discussions trying to prioritize which programs, services, and facility attributes to incorporate in a new childbirth center, Griffin recalls a poignant question raised by a board member. "If these are the programs and services women in the community are telling us they want, why not incorporate all of them?"

Once consumers were provided with the services, programs, and facilities they wanted, they came in record numbers. In only four years, the number of babies born at Griffin doubled. "The childbirth center was the start of the train," says Powanda. "After that, everything we did, every decision we made, centered around offering choices for patients and family members."

(Adapted from *Trustee*, vol. 47, no. 12, November 1996, by permission. Copyright 1996, American Hospital Publishing, Inc.)

Advocacy: On December 18, 1997, New Jersey state legislators presented Governor Christie Whitman with legislation that provided continued funding for New Jersey's Charity Care and Hospital Relief Fund programs on a permanent basis. The programs safeguard the health and well-being of all state residents by ensuring that they are guaranteed access to health care—regardless of their ability to pay. Behind the scenes were New Jersey health care trustees leading and participating in communitywide letter-writing campaigns and call-ins to state legislators on the need to find a permanent funding mechanism for charity care.

quality measurement, assessment, and improvement. They are also expected to conduct self-evaluations and participate in continuous education.

The governing board—traditionally via a quality assurance or joint conference committee—reviews the results of the quality assurance programs, asks questions, and offers its top-level support to the program. The JCAHO accreditation survey is another source of information about the quality of care provided. The survey recommendations and how the hospital is responding to the recommendations are an important source of information.

Advocacy

A final area of board operations for hospital and health care trustees lies in ongoing advocacy—in telling the organization's story. Trustees, like all change agents, can become entrenched in the assumption that the public is aware of everything the organization is doing. But a "test" that members of the American Hospital Association's Committee on Governance took in October 1996 showed just how invalid assumptions can be. Committee members were assigned to interview five people in their community to gauge public opinion on health care access, coverage, and quality. They were to use the same survey— 10 queries about the uninsured and best/worst features of the national and community health care systems. Those interviewed were to have no health care connection to the trustee.

"The purpose of the exercise was for trustees to get a different picture from the one they carry around in their heads of what health care is like in their communities," Linda Magno, the AHA's director of policy development in Washington, D.C., says in a *Trustee* magazine article. "Like many people, trustees often don't see things as they are," says trustee Carolyn B. Lewis.

Certainly that was the case for Frederic Dreyer Jr., president emeritus and honorary trustee of Charlton Health System, Fall River, Massachusetts. "I couldn't believe my ears as I talked to some of these people about access," he says. "The prevailing perception was that people without health insurance can't get medical care. It broke my heart to hear this. As not-for-profit hospitals, our mission is

> ### POINTS TO PONDER
>
> ➤ What strategies does your organization have in place to ensure and improve the quality of care? How could care be delivered differently?
>
> ➤ How could you be a better advocate for the hospital, health system, health care industry, and community? What can you do to effect change at the legislative level?

that we'll take care of you, regardless of your ability to pay." Dryer says he and others thought they were doing a good job promoting Charlton Health System's charitable mission through speaking engagements and other community outreach initiatives. "It was a real wake-up call," he says.

In a commentary appearing in *Trustee* magazine, Mary Grayson, editor of *Trustee*'s sister publication *Hospitals & Health Networks,* wrote on consumers' views of the American health care system.

"When the focus groups did mention a positive hospital experience, it generally related to a caring nurse," she writes. "How do they see hospital executives and trustees? People in the AHA's focus groups believe that skilled nurses are being systematically replaced by poorly trained, poorly paid aides. They say the profit motive is behind the thinning of nursing's ranks and that you (trustees and executives) have your priorities upside down."

With their respected and credible community-based voice and their political influence, trustees have a powerful role to play as legislative change agents. They can affect public policy and shape the future of health care delivery by joining forces via formal lobbying initiatives with their state and national hospital associations. The value of letter-writing campaigns and face-to-face meetings with legislators initiated and supported by health care trustees should never be underestimated.

Hospital Associations

On the national and state levels, hospital associations serve their members as leadership resources in the areas of advocacy, policy development, education, wellness promotion, communications, data, and research. In addition, associations offer products and services to help members operate more efficiently and cost-effectively.

In 1998, the American Hospital Association (AHA) celebrated its 100th anniversary as the leading trade association of hospitals and health systems nationwide. Its mission is to advance the health of individuals and communities by leading, representing, and serving health care provider organizations that are accountable to the community and committed to health improvement.

Several other national associations also represent certain segments of the hospital industry, such as religiously operated, not-for-profit, investor-owned, public, and specialty facilities. The AHA and these other associations (for example, the Catholic Heath Association of the United States) serve their members in several ways. Their primary role is to work with the U.S. Congress and the president's administration to promote positive public policy affecting their members and to work with regulators in federal executive branch agencies to ensure fairness in the implementation of such policy. In addition to advocacy and the shaping of public policy, these associations benefit their members by providing leadership to promote strategic directions for the field, effective communications and media relations, peer-to-peer networking opportunities, reference and referral services, educational programs, innovative resources and tools, and useful data and targeted research.

In each of the 50 states and in many metropolitan areas, there are hospital associations affiliated with, but autonomous from, the AHA. In addition to supporting the AHA's efforts at the national level, these state and local associations primarily concentrate their advocacy and policy development efforts on state legislatures, gubernatorial offices, municipal governments, and state and local regulatory agencies. Issues such as hospital licensing, building and safety codes, insurance laws, professional practice oversight, and Medicaid are matters for state and city governments. Thus, state and metropolitan hospital associations play an important role on behalf of their members.

Your hospital may be a member of several of these associations. It pays dues to support services from these organizations that would be impractical for your hospital to provide on its own. Surely, the constant legislative and regulatory challenges facing the health care community require full-time monitoring and lobbying efforts to ensure that the positions of hospitals are well researched and articulated clearly to the appropriate bodies.

Trustees are being asked increasingly to participate in the life and work of many hospital associations. These community and business leaders are serving on governance, policy development, and advisory bodies. As private citizens and volunteer activists, they are also extremely effective advocates, bringing their highly credible and politically influential voices to bear in efforts to reach policy makers with association positions.

The AHA, through its Committee on Governance and Division of Trustee and Community Leadership, and many state hospital associations, through their own delegations and programs devoted to hospital and health system governance, stand ready to serve you and your governing body in your quest for governance excellence. All trustees should take advantage of these opportunities to receive education, obtain useful resources, network with fellow trustees, and become involved in policy development and advocacy efforts on behalf of the health care organizations they govern and the communities they serve.

You can access AHA's Web site at *www.aha.org*. This site also provides information on its affiliated state and metropolitan associations.

RECOMMENDED READING

BOARD OPERATIONS

Board's Role in Strategic Planning

Coile, Russell C. "Strategic Planning for the Millennium: Creating Sustained Competitive Advantages in Tomorrow's Health Care Marketplace," *Russ Coile's Health Trends,* vol. 10, no. 2, December 1997, pp. 1, 3–6. ARTICLE.

Coile, Russell C. "Top 10 Health Care Trends for 1998: Tomorrow's Trends Will Be Consumerism, Cyberhealth and Co-Opetition," *Russ Coile's Health Trends,* vol. 10, no. 3, January 1998, pp. 1, 3–12. ARTICLE.

Executive Performance

Hofrichter, David A., and Gordon W. Hawthorne. "Governing Performance: Reexamining the Board's Role in Executive Compensation," *Trustee*, vol. 50, no. 6, June 1997, pp. 7–12. ARTICLE.

Orlikoff, James E., and Mary K. Totten. "CEO Evaluation and Compensation," *Trustee*, vol. 49, no. 1, January 1996, suppl.; 4 pp. ARTICLE.

Fiduciary Oversight

Hollis, Steven R. "Strategic and Economic Factors in the Hospital Conversion Process," *Health Affairs*, vol. 16, no. 2, March-April 1997, pp. 131–43. ARTICLE.

Weaver, Jonathan G. "A Finance Primer," in *Strategic Planning in Health Care: A Guide for Board Members,* by Ellen F. Goldman and Kevin C. Nolan (Chicago: American Hospital Publishing, Inc., 1994), pp. 97–124. [ISBN 1-55648-127-6]. BOOK CHAPTER.

Williams, Latham. "Integration Options," *Journal of Health and Hospital Law,* vol. 29, no. 2, March-April 1996, pp. 88–96. ARTICLE.

Quality/TQM

Edgman-Levitan, Susan, and Margaret Gerteis. "Measures of Quality: What Can Public Reporting Accomplish?" *Healthcare Forum Journal,* vol. 41, no. 1, January-February 1998, pp. 27, 36–37, 61. ARTICLE.

1998 Hospital Accreditation Standards (Chicago: Joint Commission on Accreditation of Healthcare Organizations, 1998). [ISBN 0-86688-575-7]. BOOK.

O'Malley, Sharon. "Total Quality Now! Putting QI on the Fast Track," *The Quality Letter,* vol. 9, no. 11, December 1997, pp. 2–10. ARTICLE.

Quality Resource Packet for Trustees (Chicago: American Hospital Publishing, Inc., 1992). [ISBN 0-87258-629-4]. BOOK.

Physician Credentialing

Orlikoff, James E., and Mary K. Totten. "The Board's Role in Medical Staff Credentialing," in *The Board's Role in Quality Care: A Practical Guide for Hospital Trustees* (Chicago: American Hospital Publishing, Inc., 1991), pp. 73–90. [ISBN 1-55648-061-X]. BOOK CHAPTER.

Rozovsky, Fay A., Lorne E. Rozovsky, and Linda M. Harpster. *Medical Staff Credentialing: A Practical Guide* (Chicago: American Hospital Publishing, Inc., 1994). [ISBN 1-55648-112-8]. BOOK.

Advocacy

Government Advocacy Guide (Princeton: New Jersey Hospital Association, 1997). BOOK.

Strenger, Ellen Weisman. "All Politics Is Local: Making Government Work for the Good of Your Community," *Trustee,* vol. 50, no. 1, January 1997, pp. 12–15. ARTICLE.

Glossary and Abbreviations

This glossary was developed by the New Jersey Hospital Association and the American Hospital Association's Division of Trustee and Community Leadership to assist health care trustees/directors in dealing with the often complex and confusing jumble of terms and descriptors applied in the field and the alphabet soup of abbreviations used by health care professionals, managers, payers, and policy-makers.* The understanding of this terminology grows ever more challenging as health care evolves and its delivery and financing become ever more complex.

We believe this publication is the most current and comprehensive glossary created to date for convenient use by health care trustees/directors. It has been designed to serve as a handy reference tool that health care governance leaders can keep close by in the boardroom or wherever their governance responsibilities may take them. It includes a broad range of terms, including those associated with managed care—the method rapidly becoming the predominant financing and delivery mechanism in the United States. A list of frequently used general health care abbreviations follows on page 134.

As editor of this edition, I hope you will find the glossary both useful and informative, and I would welcome any comments or suggestions you may have. Special thanks are expressed to my colleague Yvonne Blackburn for all her assistance in processing this wealth of definitions.

Joseph C. Isaacs
Vice-President for Trustee and Community Leadership
American Hospital Association

---

*A significant portion of this glossary is abridged from the New Jersey Hospital Associaton's *Glossary of Healthcare Terms and Abbreviations* and its *Handbook of Managed Care Terminology.* Additional definitions are derived from the *Understanding Guide to Health Care: A Glossary of Terms & Definitions,* published by the Understanding Business Press, San Francisco, California, copyright © 1996, and from *Healthcare Terms and Abbreviations for Boards and Medical Leaders,* published by The Governance Institute, La Jolla, California (n.d.).

GLOSSARY OF HEALTH CARE TERMS

Academic health center (AHC)—A university-operated grouping of programs, including a medical school, teaching hospital, and at least one other health profession school (e.g., dentistry, pharmacy, or nursing).

Academic medical center (AMC)—The coordinated organization on a university site of formal and graduate medical education, biomedical research, and patient care involving a medical school and its affiliated teaching hospital.

Access—The ability to obtain needed health care services. This can be affected by service availability, cost, coverage, acceptability to the patient, facility location, transportation, hours of operation, and waiting time.

Accreditation—The process whereby a health care organization is evaluated and determined to meet the quality-of-care standards established by an accrediting body (e.g., the Joint Commission on Accreditation of Healthcare Organizations and the National Committee for Quality Assurance).

Accreditation survey—The process used to evaluate whether a health services organization meets specified standards for accreditation.

Accrete—HCFA's term for the process of adding new Medicare enrollees to a plan. See also *Delete*.

Accrual—A technique for determining medical costs for enrollees over a set period so that money can be set aside in a claims reserve to be used for medical costs incurred during that period. Revenues recognized as services are rendered independent of when payment is received.

Accrual accounting—A descriptive accounting method that recognizes revenues as services are rendered, independent of the time when cash is actually received.

Acid test (quick ratio)—A financial ratio designed to measure liquidity by dividing "quick" assets (cash, marketable securities, and accounts receivable) by current liabilities.

Acquisition—The purchase of all or substantially all of the assets of a corporation (such as a hospital) by cash, other compensation, asset exchange, or gift of majority voting control.

Acquisition costs—Varied marketing costs within health plans primarily related to the acquisition of subscriber contracts.

Activities of daily living (ADL)—A measure of independent-living ability based on capacity of an individual to bathe, dress, use the toilet, eat, and move across a small room without assistance and used to determine the need for nursing home and other care.

Actuarial analysis—A means of measuring the statistical probability of the risk of events occurring, such as illness, injury, disability, hospitalization, or death.

Actuary—An accredited insurance mathematician trained in the science of loss contingencies, investments, insurance accounting, premiums, managed care risks, and service utilization who calculates premium rates, reserves, and dividends.

Acute care—A term that generally refers to short-term inpatient hospital care of fewer than 30 days.

Adjusted average per capita cost (AAPCC)—The methodology used to develop the premium rate paid to HMOs for Medicare enrollees in a geographic region, based on a county-level estimate of the average cost incurred by Medicare for each beneficiary in fee-for-service care and adjusted by the level of spending that would occur if each county contained the same mix of beneficiaries. This estimate is calculated by multiplying outpatient visits by the ratio of outpatient charges per visit to inpatient charges per admission.

Adjusted community rating (ACR)—A procedure used to determine and set group rates for the expected use of health care services during an upcoming contract period (usually one year). The ACR is based on a group's prior use of health care services and is used to forecast the group's use of services relative to the average use for all members in a plan.

Adjusted patient day (APD)—An accounting method for modifying the definition of inpatient days to include outpatient revenues.

Administrative costs—The costs assumed by a health care organization, insurer, or managed care plan for managing health services, including claims processing, billing, marketing, member services, provider relations, and other overhead expenses.

Administrative services only (ASO) contract—A contract that requires a third party to provide only administrative services (e.g., claims processing, actuarial support, or employee communications) to large employers that self insure for their employees' health coverage.

Admission—The formal acceptance of a patient into a hospital or other inpatient or extended care setting for the purpose of providing care.

Admitting privileges—The authorization given to a provider by a health care organization's governing board to admit patients into its hospital or health care facility to provide patient care. Privileges are based on the provider's license, education, training, and experience.

Adult day care/adult day health care (ADHC)—Programs providing social, recreational, or other activities specifically for elderly people who cannot be left alone or do not wish to be left alone during the day while their family members work. It combines day care with certain health care services.

Advance directive—An individual's written instructions recognized under state law, either in the form of a living will or durable power of attorney for health care, and related to the provision of health care when he or she is completely incapacitated.

Adverse drug reaction—A negative physical reaction or complication caused by the use of a medication(s).

Adverse selection—A term referring to specific plans or insurance options being adversely affected by enrolling large proportions of persons with higher risk or poorer health status, causing higher-than-average costs. See also *Favorable selection.*

Affiliation—An agreement, usually formal, between two or more otherwise independent hospitals, programs, or providers describing their relationship to each other.

Aftercare—Posthospitalization care and treatment of a convalescent patient.

Against medical advice (AMA)—Decision by a patient and/or his or her family to ignore the counsel of physicians regarding care of the patient.

Agency for Health Care Policy and Research (AHCPR)—A federal agency responsible for research on quality, appropriateness, effectiveness, and cost of health care and for using these data to promote improvement in clinical practice and the organization, financing, and delivery of health care.

Alliance—A formal organization or association owned by shareholders or controlled by members that works on behalf of the common interests of its individual members in the provision of services and products and in the promotion of activities and ventures.

Allied health professional—A specially trained nonphysician health care provider. Allied health professionals include: paramedics, physician's assistants (PAs), certified nurse midwives (CNMs) nurse practitioners (NPs), and other caregivers who perform tasks that supplement physician services.

Allowed charge—The amount Medicare approves for payment to a physician, typically reimbursing for a proportion of this charge, with the beneficiary paying the remainder.

All-payer system—A system by which the government sets pay rates for all payers of health care bills, including the government, private insurers, large companies, and individuals.

Alternative delivery system (ADS)—Nontraditional nonindemnity health insurance programs such as HMOs and PPOs that both finance and provide health care for their members.

Ambulatory—A term describing a patient who does not need to be confined to a bed and is capable of moving about from place to place.

Ambulatory care—Health services provided on an outpatient basis.

Ambulatory care group (ACG)—A term referring to the method of categorizing outpatient episodes using 51 mutually exclusive groupings based on resource use over time and modified by principal diagnosis, age, and sex.

Ambulatory patient classifications (APC)—A method of classifying outpatient episodes.

Ambulatory diagnostic group (ADG)—A term referring to the method of categorizing outpatient episodes into 34 possible groupings.

Ambulatory patient group (APG)—A term referring to an outpatient services reimbursement methodology created for the HCFA for use in Medicare programs.

Ambulatory surgical center (ASC)—A freestanding facility, often certified by Medicare, that performs certain types of surgical procedures on an outpatient basis.

Ancillary services—Support services and procedures offered in hospitals or outpatient settings, such as laboratory, radiology, and pharmacy services.

Antitrust laws—State and national laws that prohibit health care and other providers from price-fixing or developing monopolies that would prevent consumers from having choices in terms of costs and services.

Any willing provider—(1) Any health care provider that complies with an insurer's preferred provider terms and conditions and may thus apply for and receive designation as a preferred provider. (2) A reference to legislation compelling insurers to sign a participation agreement with any provider that agrees to abide by the same terms of the contract and accept the same payment level as other providers.

Appropriateness review—A methodology in which individual cases are evaluated for clinical appropriateness and for medical necessity of surgical and diagnostic procedures. The review usually consists of comparing clinical data to medical criteria.

Arbitration—The process by which a contractual dispute is submitted to a mutually agreed-on impartial party for resolution. Many managed care plans have provisions for compulsory arbitration (in states where arbitration is allowed) in cases of disputes between providers and plans.

Assignment—An agreement by a physician to bill Medicare directly and receive the "allowed charge" as full payment for services rendered. Other third-party payers may have similar arrangements on a "reasonable-charge" basis. See also *Nonparticipating physician or provider.*

Assisted living facilities—Living arrangements for the elderly and disabled who need assistance with daily living activities such as dressing, bathing, and cooking.

Attending physician—The hospital medical staff member legally responsible for the care provided to a given patient.

Authorization—A utilization management technique used by managed care organizations to grant approval for the provision of care or services not performed by the primary care physician. Services requiring authorization vary greatly by health plan.

Auxilian—A member of a hospital's auxiliary who may or may not serve as an in-service volunteer at the hospital.

Average daily census (ADC)—The average number of hospital inpatients per day over a given period that is calculated by dividing the total number of patient days during a given period by the number of calendar days in that period.

Average length of stay (ALOS)—The total number of hospital bed days divided by the number of admissions or discharges during a specified period.

Bad debt—Charges for care provided to patients who are financially able to pay but refuse to do so.

Balance billing—The practice under Medicare and private fee-for-service health insurance of billing patients for the portion of charges not approved by the health plan. Under Medicare fee-for-service, a balance bill cannot exceed 15 percent of the allowed charge for nonparticipating physicians. See also *Out-of-pocket expenditures.*

Balanced Budget Act of 1997 (BBA)—A law that initiated a new Children's Health Insurance Program (CHIP) and made changes to Medicare reimbursement in such areas as home health and transfers.

Bar code—A printed array of bars of contrasting widths and spaces encoded with machine-readable information used to identify materials (e.g., x rays, specimens, and medical records) coming into or generated by hospitals.

Basic health care services—Health care services that an enrolled population might reasonably require to maintain good health, including as a minimum emergency care, inpatient hospital and medical services, and outpatient medical services.

Bed conversion—Reallocation of beds from one type of care (e.g., acute care) to another (long-term care). See also *Swing beds.*

Bed days—The total number of days of hospital care (excluding the day of discharge) provided to the insured or plan member. Bed days, also called *hospital days, discharge days,* or *patient days,* are used to measure hospital utilization and are generally reported in "days per 1,000 plan members per year."

Benchmarking—The process of continually measuring products, services, and practices against major competitors or industry leaders to create normative or comparative standards (benchmarks).

Beneficiary—Someone eligible to receive benefits under an insurance policy or coverage plan.

Benefit levels—The limit or degree of services to which a person is entitled based on his or her contract with a health plan or insurer.

Benefit(s) package—Services an insurer, government agency, or health plan offers to a group or individual under the terms of a contract, typically outlined in the written evidence of coverage (EOC).

Best practices—A term describing organizations' superior performance in their operational, managerial, and/or clinical processes.

Billed charges—A reimbursement method used mostly by traditional indemnity insurance companies wherein charges for health care services are billed on a fee-for-service basis. Fees are based on what the provider typically charges all patients for the particular service.

Biomedical ethics—An area of study addressing philosophical questions regarding morals, values, and ethics in the provision of health care.

Birthing rooms—Homelike hospital-based combination labor and delivery units in which new mothers and fathers can participate in the childbirth process.

Block grants—A program funding approach wherein the federal government makes lump-sum grants to states, which are then responsible for determining beneficiary eligibility, managing the program, and contributing matching funds.

The Blues—Common slang for Blue Cross and Blue Shield plans.

Board certified—The term describing a physician who has passed the national certifying examination of a medical specialty board to demonstrate that his or her knowledge and clinical skills meet specific standards in a particular field or specialty such as anesthesiology, radiology, or internal medicine.

Board eligible—The term referring to the period when a physician may take a specialty board examination for certification after graduating from a board-approved medical school, completing an accredited training program, and practicing for a specified length of time.

Brain death—Total irreversible cessation of cerebral function as well as cessation of spontaneous function of the respiratory and circulatory systems.

Bundled billing—The practice of charging an all-inclusive package price for all medical services associated with selected procedures (e.g., heart surgery or maternity care) to improve quality and help control costs. Also called a *package price*. See also *Global fee.*

Bundled case rate—A single per case payment for both hospital and physician charges.

Business coalitions on health—Voluntary organizations of mostly self-insured employers, employer associations, and other groups concerned about health care costs and active in developing cost-containment strategies.

Cafeteria benefits—See *Flexible benefits.*

Capital—Owner's equity in a business and often used to mean the total assets of a business, although sometimes used to describe working capital (i.e., cash) available for investment or acquisition of goods.

Capital asset—Depreciable property of a fixed or permanent nature (e.g., buildings and equipment) that is not for sale in the regular course of business.

Capital expenditure review—An internal or regulatory evaluation of a health care facility's planned capital expenditures (e.g., buildings and equipment) to determine their necessity and appropriateness.

Capital expense—An expenditure that benefits more than one accounting period, such as the cost to acquire long-term assets.

Capital structure—The permanent long-term financing of an organization: the relative proportions of short-term debt, long-term debt, and owners' equity.

Capital structure (leverage)—Measure of the extent to which debt financing is employed by a corporation; the mix of long-term debt and equity employed by a corporation for permanent, long-term financing needs.

Capitalize—To record an expenditure (e.g., R&D costs) that may benefit a future period as an asset rather than as an expense of the period of its occurrence.

Capitation—A risk-sharing method of payment for health services in which a provider is paid a fixed (typically monthly) amount for each plan enrollee/patient served regardless of the services provided to each patient. These rates may vary by age and sex of the patient/plan enrollee. See also *Group model HMO; Health maintenance organization (HMO); Independent practice association (IPA) model HMO; Staff model HMO.*

Caps—Maximum allowable limits placed on revenue or rates by the federal or state government.

Captive insurance companies—Typically, a wholly owned subsidiary of a group of hospitals that have organized to insure their risk.

Care—The provision of accommodations, comfort, and treatments to an individual, implying responsibility for safety.

Carrier—An insurance company or a health plan that has some financial risk or that manages health care benefits.

Carve-out benefits/service—Specific benefits or services (e.g., mental health, substance abuse, dental, and vision benefits) that are financed and administered separately from the rest of an organization's basic health insurance package. These may also be referred to as *clinical exclusion.*

Case management—A system of assessment, treatment planning, referral, and follow-up that ensures the provision of services according to a patient's needs and the coordination of payment and reimbursement for care.

Case manager (CM)—A professional (usually a nurse, physician, or social worker) who handles specific catastrophic or high-cost cases as a member of a utilization management team. Case managers work together with patients, providers, and insurers to coordinate a plan to provide medically and clinically appropriate health care, control costs, and monitor the patient's progress.

Case mix—A measure of patient acuity reflecting different patients' needs for hospital resources. This measure may be based on patients' diagnoses, the severity of their illnesses, and their utilization of services. A high case-mix index refers to a patient population more ill than average. See also *Patient mix.*

Case-mix severity—Level of illness or disability within a particular case-mix grouping. Also referred to as *severity of illness.*

Case rate—A reimbursement model that establishes a flat admission rate for all the services associated with all care immediately before and after diagnosis of a condition.

Catastrophic illness—Any acute or prolonged illness that is usually considered to be life-threatening or may produce serious residual disability, entailing substantial expense over an extended period.

Catastrophic insurance—(1) Insurance that protects the insured against all or a percentage of costs not covered by other insurance or prepayment plans or incurred under specified circumstances. (2) Insurance in excess of specified dollar or benefit amounts or limits.

Catchment area—Geographic area defined and served by a hospital and delineated on the basis of such factors as population distribution, natural geographic boundaries, or transportation accessibility.

Categorical funding—Funding for government programs to groups of people who qualify based on some category of services, such as Social Security disability, developmental disability, or AFDC. Under some Medicaid reform proposals, all categorical funding would be eliminated and each state would receive matching block grants and decide who receives which particular services.

Census—The average number of inpatients, excluding newborns, receiving care each day during a reported period.

Center of excellence (COE)—A specialized product line (e.g., neurosciences, cardiac services, or orthopedics) developed by a provider to be a recognized high-quality, high-volume, cost-effective clinical program.

Centers for Disease Control and Prevention (CDC)—A division of the U.S. Public Health Service that takes the lead in analyzing and fighting infectious diseases.

Certificate of authority (COA)—A license to operate an HMO within a state issued by the state government. In most states, COAs are issued by the Department of Insurance; however, in California they are issued by the Department of Corporations.

Certificate of coverage—The legal description listing the benefits, providers, and general rules and regulations of the health plan given to employees or beneficiaries.

Certificate of need (CON)—A document for the purpose of cost control granted by a state to a hospital seeking permission to modify its facility, acquire major medical equipment, or offer a new or different health service on the basis of need.

Charges—The amount billed by a hospital for services provided. A charge generally includes the cost plus an operating margin. Many payers pay a discounted rate, negotiated rate, or government-set rate.

Charity care—See *Indigent care.*

Chase and pay—See *Pursue and pay.*

Chemical dependency—Alcohol or drug addiction. Services that fight these addictions are called chemical dependence services or substance abuse services.

Chemical equivalents—Medications that have basically the same chemicals as a brand-name drug and must meet FDA standards in order to be sold or marketed.

Cherry picking—The practice of insurance companies of accepting only those businesses, occupations, companies, or individuals with minimal health risks and avoiding businesses or people that are riskier. See also *Skimming.*

Chief executive officer (CEO)—The individual appointed by an organization's governing board to be its top staff person directing the organization's overall management.

Chief of staff—Member of a hospital medical staff who is elected, appointed, or employed by the hospital to be the medical and administrative head of the medical staff.

Childbirth center—A freestanding or hospital-based facility that provides prenatal, childbirth, and postnatal care, often incorporating family-centered maternity care concepts and practices.

Children's Health Insurance Program (CHIP)—A program enacted within the Balanced Budget Act of 1997 providing federal matching funds to states to help expand health care coverage for children under Medicaid or new programs.

Chronic care—Both medical care and services that are not directly medical related, such as cooking, giving medications, and bathing, for those with chronic illnesses.

Chronic illness—A condition (e.g., Alzheimer's disease, diabetes, and epilepsy) that will not improve substantially, lasts a lifetime, or recurs and may require long-term care.

Churning—The unethical practice in a fee-for-service reimbursement environment of a provider seeing a patient more often than is medically necessary in order to increase revenue.

Civilian Health and Medical Program of the Uniformed Services (CHAMPUS)—A health plan that serves the dependents of active-duty military personnel and retired military personnel and their dependents. Retired military personnel over age 65 use Medicare instead of CHAMPUS.

Claim—Information submitted in writing or electronically by providers to an insurer requesting payment for medical services provided to the beneficiary.

Claims-made coverage/policy—A form of liability coverage for claims made (reported or filed) against an insured party during the policy period irrespective of when the event occurred that caused the claims to be made. Thus, claims made during a previous period in which the policyholder was insured under a claims-made policy would be covered, provided the coverage is continuous with the insurer.

Claims pooling—A technique in which claims are "pooled" to obtain an average claims experience for the covered group. For example, claims pooling may be used to determine the premium for a group risk based on the average claims experience of the membership.

Claims review—The method by which an enrollee's health care service claims are reviewed before reimbursement is made. Review involves a routine examination of a submitted claim to determine eligibility, coverage of services, and plan liability.

Clinic without walls—See *Group practice without walls.*

Clinical exclusion—See *Carve-out benefits/service.*

Clinical pathway—A treatment regimen agreed to by a consensus of clinicians. Only essential elements—components that directly affect care—are part of the clinical pathway. See also *Critical pathway.*

Clinician—A health care professional who is directly involved with patient care.

Closed access—A term describing an HMO that requires its members to seek care from network providers through a primary care physician to receive benefits and that does not provide benefits for out-of-network care.

Closed formulary—A list restricting the number and type of drugs covered by a pharmacy benefits management program or managed care plan.

Closed panel—A managed care plan that contracts with or employs physicians on an exclusive basis for services and does not allow those physicians to see patients from other managed care organizations. Staff model HMOs are examples of closed-panel managed care plans. See also *Open staff.*

Closed staff—A hospital's medical staff that accepts no new applicants or a physician or physician group that exclusively provides under contract all the administrative and clinical services required for operation of a hospital department.

Code blue/code Leo—The terms used to indicate that an emergency situation has occurred in the hospital and that mobilizes staff to respond.

Code creep—The practice of billing for more intensive services than were actually provided for which a higher payment is received.

Code of Federal Regulations—A codified collection of regulations issued by various departments, bureaus, and agencies of the federal government and promulgated in the *Federal Register.*

Coinsurance—A cost-sharing technique in a health insurance policy requiring the insured to pay an amount for medical and hospital services after payment of a deductible. See also *Out-of-pocket expenditures.*

Commercial carrier—A for-profit private insurance carrier (e.g., Aetna, CIGNA, and Prudential) that offers health and other types of coverage.

Commission on Professional and Hospital Activities (CPHA)—A private not-for-profit organization established in 1955 for the purpose of collecting, analyzing, and distributing hospital-use data based on medical record discharge abstracts.

Commissions—Fees charged by and paid to insurance agents and brokers for their role in selling a particular health plan to a company or an individual. Commissions are included in health care premiums and are considered an administrative expense.

Community—The geographic, demographic, or socioeconomic designation of a health care organization's service area.

Community accountability—The responsibility of providers in a network to document to members (or enrollees) their progress toward specific community health goals and their maintenance of specific clinical standards.

Community benefits—Activities initiated by not-for-profit hospitals to benefit the hospital's community. Community benefits are evolving standards defined by the Internal Revenue Service (IRS) to determine the tax-exempt status of not-for-profit health care organizations.

Community care network (CCN)—Collaborative relationships among a set of local providers organized on a community level and paid on a capitated basis to deliver an enrolled population a broad scope of cost-effective services across an integrated continuum of care. [Community Care Network, Inc., uses the name Community Care Network as its service mark and reserves all rights—Ed.]

Community health (needs) assessment—A dynamic process undertaken to identify a community's health status, problems, and goals, enabling the establishment of communitywide health priorities and facilitating collaborative action planning directed toward improving the community's health status. The process involves multiple sectors of the community.

Community health center—A local, community-based ambulatory health care program, also known as a neighborhood health center, organized and funded by the U.S. Public Health Service to provide primary and preventive health services, particularly in areas with scarce health resources and/or special-needs populations. Some are sponsored by local hospitals and/or community foundations.

Community Health Information Network (CHIN)—The linkage of health care vendors, doctors, hospitals, and health plans using the same computer programs and methods to collect and store data and transfer information. It is designed to reduce paperwork and, as a result, health care costs as well as to improve the quality of care by making it possible to compare such information as health outcomes and costs in a specific community.

Community physician-hospital organization (CPHO)—An organization composed of physicians, hospitals, and their medical staff as well as community health and human services in a community. It can contract with managed care plans to provide services.

Community rating—A method for calculating health insurance premiums based on the average cost of the actual or anticipated health services used by all subscribers in a specific geographic area or industry. This method spreads the cost of illness evenly over all subscribers rather than charging the sick more than the healthy.

Comorbidity—A preexisting patient condition that, linked to a principal diagnosis, causes an increase in length of stay by at least one day in approximately 75 percent of cases.

Competitive medical plan (CMP)—A federal designation that allows a health plan to obtain a Medicare risk contract without having to obtain qualification as an HMO. Requirements for eligibility are somewhat less restrictive than those for an HMO.

Compliance—The act of conforming with stated requirements, such as standards; it may be measured in a range from noncompliance to full compliance.

Comprehensive health care—Services that meet the total health care needs of a patient.

Comprehensive outpatient rehabilitation facility (CORF)—A hospital-based outpatient facility providing a full range of rehabilitative services.

Computerized axial tomography (CAT or CT) scanner—Diagnostic equipment that produces cross-sectional images of the head and body by means of computer synthesis of x-ray particles.

Concurrent review—A managed care technique in which a managed care firm continuously reviews the charts of hospitalized patients for appropriate lengths of stay and treatment.

Confidentiality—(1) Restriction of access to data and information to individuals who have a need, reason, and permission for such access. (2) An individual's right, within the law, to personal and informational privacy, including his or her health care records.

Consolidated Omnibus Budget Reconciliation Act of 1985 (COBRA)—A federal law that requires employers with more than 20 employees to extend group health insurance coverage for at least 18 months after employees leave their jobs. Employees must pay 102 percent of the premium.

Consolidation—The unification of two or more corporations by their dissolution and creation of a single new corporation.

Consortium—A formal voluntary alliance of institutions for a specific purpose, functioning under a common set of bylaws or rules. Unless otherwise proscribed, each member controls its own assets.

Consultation—The act within medical practice of requesting advice from another provider, usually a specialist, regarding a patient's diagnosis or treatment.

Consumer price index, medical care component—An inflationary measure encompassing the cost of all purchased health care services.

Continuing care—Care provided over an extended period of time in various settings, spanning the illness-to-wellness continuum.

Continuing care retirement communities—A residential setting for retirees offering a range of services from independent living to assisted living and sometimes nursing home care.

Continuing education (CE)—Education beyond initial professional preparation that is relevant to the type of care delivered. Such education provides current knowledge relevant to an individual's field of practice or service responsibilities and may be related to findings from performance-improvement activities.

Continuing medical education (CME)—Continuing education related to the current practices of physicians.

Continuity/continuum of care—A comprehensive set of services ranging from preventive and ambulatory services to acute care to long-term, rehabilitative, and hospice services. Prevention and early intervention are emphasized for high-risk patients, and the transition between services is made easier as needs change.

Continuous quality improvement (CQI)—The process at the heart of the total quality management philosophy that views quality as never static but rather as a constantly moving target always open to improvement through systematic evaluation and modification of processes and services. See also *Quality improvement program (QIP)*.

Contract management—Daily management of an organization under contract by another organization, wherein the managed organization retains legal responsibility and ownership of the facility's assets and liabilities and the managing organization typically reports directly to the managed organization's board or owners.

Contractual adjustment—A bookkeeping adjustment to reflect uncollectible differences between established charges for services to insured persons and rates payable for those services under contracts with third-party payers.

Contractual allowances—Negotiated discounts on hospital or other provider-established charges paid by third-party payers or the government.

Conversion—(1) A major change that a hospital undertakes, such as the conversion from not-for-profit status to for-profit or the conversion of an acute care facility to ambulatory care, and usually entailing a complete change of mission after a new line of business or service displaces a core activity. (2) A reference to the transfer of a plan member covered under a group contract (such as a contract with a large employer) to coverage under an individual contract without evidence of medical insurability after termination of the group coverage.

Cooperative/co-op—(1) A type of health maintenance organization that is managed by the members of the health plan. (2) An insurance-purchasing arrangement in which businesses or other groups join together to gain the buying power of large employers or groups.

Coordination of benefits (COB)—Agreement between health plans and insurers to avoid the same services being paid for more than once.

Copayment—A cost-sharing arrangement in which a fixed dollar amount is paid for a covered service by a health insurance enrollee (e.g., $10 for a physician's office visit). See also *Out-of-pocket expenditures.*

Corporate diversification—Organizational restructuring that broadens revenue-generating activities and services through the creation of new corporations, limited partnerships, foundations, and joint ventures to provide alternative services.

Corporate practice of medicine restriction—A state law that prohibits a physician from contracting with a corporation that is not a professional corporation.

Corporate restructuring—The formation and use of one or more corporations in addition to the hospital corporation for the purpose of holding assets or carrying out other business activities. Restructuring generally involves either the formation of corporations legally independent of the hospital or the hospital becoming a subsidiary of a new parent corporate structure.

Cost accounting—An accounting system arriving at charges by health care providers based on actual costs for services rendered.

Cost-benefit analysis—A method comparing the costs of a project to the resulting benefits, usually expressed in monetary value.

Cost center—A business or organizational unit of activity or responsibility that incurs expenses.

Cost containment—Control or reduction of inefficiencies in the consumption, allocation, or production of health services that contributes to the high cost of health care.

Cost finding—Determining how much it actually costs to provide a given service—usually requiring a cost-accounting system or a retrospective cost study.

Cost sharing—Payments made by health insurance enrollees for covered services. Examples include deductibles, coinsurance, and copayments.

Cost shifting—Increasing charges to one group of patients (e.g., revenues from commercial insurers) to offset losses from other groups of patients (e.g., lower net payments from Medicare).

Cost-to-charge ratio—A cost-finding measure derived from applying the ratio of third-party payer charges to total charges against the total operating costs in a hospital operating department.

Covered lives—The total number of people in a health plan or the people covered by an insurer.

Covered services—Specific health care services and supplies for which payers provide reimbursement under the terms of the applicable contract (Medicaid, Medicare, group contract, or individual subscriber contract).

Credentialing—A process by which a hospital determines the scope of practice of practitioners providing services in the hospital; criteria for granting privileges or credentialing are determined by the hospital and include individual character, competence, training, experience, and judgment. Also called *privileging.*

Credentialing verification organization (CVO)—An independent organization that confirms the professional credentials of providers for a managed care organization rather than requiring the providers to provide this information independently.

Critical-access hospital (CAH)—Designated within the Medicare Rural Hospital Flexibility Program as a limited service rural, not-for-profit, or public hospital that provides outpatient and short-term inpatient hospital care on an urgent or emergency basis and is a part of a rural health network.

Critical pathway—A health care management tool based on clinical consensus on the best way to treat a disease or use a procedure and designed to reduce variations in health care procedures. See also *Clinical pathway.*

Current assets—Assets that are expected to be turned into cash within one year (e.g., accounts receivable).

Current liabilities—Obligations that will become due and payable with cash within one year.

Current Procedural Terminology (CPT)—A classification system that is the basis for determining the costs of specific health care services and procedures. Each service procedure has a five-digit code. CPT, in its fourth edition, is an industry standard for coding and billing.

Current ratio—A financial ratio designed to measure liquidity based on the relationship or balance between current assets and current liabilities.

Custodial care—Basic long-term care, also called *personal care,* for someone with a terminal or chronic illness.

Customary, prevailing, and reasonable (CPR)—Criteria used by Medicare for setting the approved charge for a Medicare Part B service from a specific physician or supplier. Using the CPR criteria, the lowest of the following three charges is approved: the physician's actual charge for the service, the physician's customary charge for the service, or the charge used by peer providers in the same geographical area. See also *Reasonable and customary charge.*

Days per thousand—A standard unit of hospital utilization measurement that refers to the annualized use (in days) of hospital or other institutional care for each 1,000 covered lives.

Dead on arrival (DOA)—The arrival at a hospital of a deceased patient.

Death rate (hospital-based)—Number of deaths of inpatients in relation to the total number of inpatients over a given period of time.

Death spiral—An insurance term that refers to a vicious spiral of high premium rates and adverse selection, generally in a free-choice environment.

Deductible—The amount of expense a covered or insured person must initially pay, typically in a calendar year, before the health plan will make payment for eligible benefits. See also *Out-of-pocket expenditures.*

Deemed status—A term used to describe the condition of a hospital deemed qualified to participate in the Medicare program if it is accredited by the JCAHO, thus obviating the need for a duplicative Medicare accreditation survey.

Defensive medicine—Health care under which providers order more tests than necessary to protect themselves from potential lawsuits by patients and said to be a major reason health care costs are so high, particularly under fee-for-service medicine.

Delegated authorities—An integrated delivery network to which a managed care organization has delegated the responsibility for providing such services as credentialing, billing, and quality assurance.

Delete—HCFA's term for the process of removing Medicare enrollees from a plan. See also *Accrete.*

Demand management—The range of customer services that health plans provide to members, including calls welcoming them to the health plan, the scheduling of patient appointments, and patient tracking and referral services. These services can include 24-hour phone lines, nurse referrals, and member education.

Denial—The refusal by a third-party payer to either reimburse a provider for services or authorize payment for services prospectively. Denials are generally issued on the basis that a hospital admission, diagnostic test, treatment, or continued stay is inappropriate according to a set of guidelines.

Dental health maintenance organization (DHMO)—An HMO organized strictly to provide dental benefits.

Dependent—A member of a health plan by virtue of a family relationship with the member who has the health plan coverage.

Diagnosis-related groups (DRGs)—Groups in a system used by Medicare for classifying hospital patients based on their clinical condition (diagnosis or surgical procedure), age, and whether they had any other illnesses (complications or comorbidities); a predetermined price is set for each of almost 500 mutually exclusive DRGs.

Diagnostic and Statistical Manual of Mental Disorders, 3rd edition, revised (DSM III-R)—The manual used to provide a diagnostic coding system for mental and substance abuse disorders.

Diagnostic test—An examination or procedure (such as a urine test for pregnancy) that is used to determine a person's particular illness, disease, or condition.

Differentiated oligopoly—A situation in which the market is affected by a small number of interconnected businesses whose products, while not the same, are similar.

Direct contracting—An agreement between a hospital and a corporate purchaser for the delivery of health care services at a certain price. A third party may be included to provide administrative and financial services.

Directors' and officers' (D&O) liability coverage—Insurance protection for directors and officers of corporations against suits or claims brought by shareholders or others alleging that the directors and/or officers acted improperly in some manner in the conduct of their duties. This coverage does not extend to dishonest acts.

Discharge planning—The evaluation of patients' medical needs in order to arrange for appropriate care after discharge from an inpatient setting.

Discharges—The number of patients who leave an overnight medical care facility (usually a hospital but occasionally an extended care facility).

Discounted fee-for-service—A common risk-sharing payment method similar to fee-for-service except that the amount of money a provider charges for its health services is discounted based on a negotiated amount or percentage that is agreed on between the provider and the health plan.

Disease management—The process in which a physician or clinical team coordinates treatment and manages a patient's chronic disease (such as asthma or epilepsy) on a long-term, continuing basis, rather than providing single episodic treatments.

Disenrollment—The voluntary or involuntary termination of an enrollee's coverage under a health plan.

Disincentive plan—A health plan in which the member is discouraged from using a provider that is not in the plan's network. If the member uses a nonnetwork provider, the level of current benefits is reduced (or copayments and deductibles increased).

Disproportionate share (DSH) adjustment—A payment adjustment under Medicare's prospective payment system or under Medicaid for hospitals that serve a large volume of low-income patients.

Doctor—A term that refers to a variety of people in the health care system, including MDs, doctors of naturopathy, doctors of chiropractic, and doctors of psychology. It does not necessarily mean physician.

Do not resuscitate (DNR) order—An order placed on a patient's chart by the attending physician, with patient or surrogate consent, that directs hospital personnel not to revive the patient if respiratory or cardiac activity ceases.

Dread disease—A type of insurance sold as a protection against a particular disease, such as cancer or heart disease.

DRG creep—The prohibited practice of classifying patients at a higher level of severity in order for a health care provider to receive higher Medicare payments.

Drive-by deliveries/drive-through deliveries—A slang reference to the practice of many health plans and insurance companies to limit hospital stays for a normal birth to 24 hours. The U.S. Congress and several states have enacted so-called baby bills that would allow the mother and infant to stay up to 48 hours for a normal delivery and up to 72 hours for a cesarean delivery.

Drug Enforcement Administration (DEA)—The federal agency that licenses individuals to prescribe medications.

Drug formulary—A list of prescription drugs covered by an insurance plan or used within a hospital. A positive formulary lists eligible products while a negative one lists exclusions. Some insurers will not reimburse for prescribed drugs not listed on the formulary; others may have limited reimbursement for nonformulary drugs.

Drug price review (DPR)—The monthly updates of the average wholesale price (AWP) of prescription drugs from the American Druggist Blue Book.

Drug utilization review (DUR)—An evaluation of customer drug use and cost patterns at all stages, including the prescribing and dispensing of the drug, in order to determine the effectiveness and appropriateness of prescribed drug therapy.

Dual choice—A term that usually refers to the federal HMO regulation (section 1310) requiring companies meeting certain criteria to offer a federally qualified HMO as a health plan option. See also *Dual option.*

Dual option—The offering of both an HMO and a traditional indemnity insurance plan by one carrier. See also *Dual choice.*

Durable medical equipment (DME)—A classification of equipment that includes wheelchairs, artificial limbs, and other nondisposable equipment. Only certain DME is covered by insurance or public programs.

Durable power of attorney for health care—A legal instrument that allows individuals to designate in advance another person to act on their behalf if they are unable to make a decision to accept, maintain, discontinue, or refuse any health care services.

Economies of scale—Rewards of efficiency and cost savings resulting from mass production.

Effectiveness—The degree to which care is provided in the correct manner, given the current state of knowledge, to achieve the desired or projected outcome(s).

Efficacy—The degree to which the care of the individual has been shown to accomplish the desired or projected outcome(s).

Efficiency—The relationship between the outcomes (results of care) and the resources used to deliver care.

Elective—A health care procedure that is not an emergency and that the patient and doctor plan in advance, such as knee replacement or prostate surgery.

Eligibility—The status that defines who receives health care services and benefits and for what period of time they qualify to use those benefits.

Eligibility verification—The process of confirming that a person is a subscriber to a health plan, which, in some HMOs, means confirming the member's benefit plan and copayment responsibilities.

Emergency medical services system (EMS)—A system of personnel, facilities, and equipment administered by a public or not-for-profit organization delivering emergency medical services within a designated geographic area.

Emergency Medical Treatment and Active Labor Act (EMTALA)—Also known as the *"antidumping" provision* under COBRA, legislation requiring that all patients who come to the emergency department of a hospital must receive an appropriate medical screening exam regardless of ability to pay and be stabilized if they are to be transferred to another facility.

Emergency preparedness plan—A process designed to manage the consequences of natural disasters or other major emergency disruptions to the ability to provide care and treatment.

Employee assistance programs (EAPs)—Programs under which employers contract with companies to provide alcohol, substance abuse, and other mental health services for their employees if these services are not covered under their employee health care benefits.

Employee Retirement Income Security Act of 1974 (ERISA)—Legislation that permits, among many other things, large employers to self-insure their employee health care benefits and to be exempt from any state insurance regulations and premium taxes. Companies covered under ERISA are exempt from state insurance regulations and health care legislation. Many states need waivers to ERISA to implement some of their legislated reforms.

Employer mandate—A requirement that employers pay part or all of their employees' health insurance premiums. Under an employer mandate, employees get their health insurance through their company rather than buying it individually or having the government pay for it in a tax-based or single-payer system.

Encounter—A record of a medically related service (or visit) rendered by a provider to a health plan enrollee typically using a standard billing form or an HMO-specific encounter form.

Endowment fund—The principal or original investment maintained in a permanent fund to provide income for general or restricted uses of an agency, institution, or program.

End-stage renal disease (ESRD)—Late stage of kidney disease requiring frequent blood dialysis and eventually organ transplantation; dialysis is covered under a special federal program.

Enrollee—See *Member.*

Enrollment—(1) The total number of covered persons (i.e., the enrolled group) in a health plan. (2) The process by which a health plan signs up individuals and groups for membership. See also *Open enrollment period.*

Entitlements—Programs in which people receive services and benefits based on some specific criteria, such as income or age. Examples of entitlement programs include Medicaid, Medicare, and veterans' benefits.

Environmental assessment—A planning method involving identification of the major external factors expected to present opportunities and/or problems over the planning period and an analysis of the operational implications of those factors on the organization.

Episode of care—The collection of all medical and pharmaceutical services rendered to a patient for a given illness, disease, or injury, across all settings of care (inpatient, outpatient, ambulatory) and across providers, for the duration of that illness.

Equity model—A form of for-profit health care delivery system in which the physicians or other providers are owners.

Ethics committee—A multidisciplinary group that convenes for the purpose of staff education and policy development in areas related to the use and limitation of aggressive medical technology. It also acts as a resource to patients, family, staff, physicians, and clergy regarding health care options surrounding terminal illness and assists with living wills.

Evidence of coverage (EOC)—Any certificate, agreement, contract, brochure, or letter of entitlement issued to a subscriber or enrollee setting forth the coverage to which the subscriber or enrollee is entitled.

Excess capacity—The difference between the number of hospital beds being used for patient care and the number of beds available.

Excess risk insurance—See *Reinsurance; Stop-loss insurance.*

Exclusions—Medical conditions specified in an insurance policy for which the insurer will provide no benefits.

Exclusive contract—An agreement that gives a physician or physician group the right to provide all administrative and clinical services required for the operation of a hospital department and precludes other physicians from practicing that specialty in that institution for the period of the contract.

Exclusive multiple option (EMO)—An arrangement made by an employer wherein an insurance carrier or managed care plan provides and coordinates a comprehensive package of plans that may include any combination of indemnity insurance, HMO, PPO, or POS plans. In exchange, the employer agrees that the carrier will be the sole vendor for coverage of eligible employees.

Exclusive provider organization (EPO)—A health care payment and delivery arrangement in which members must obtain all their care from doctors and hospitals within an established network; benefits are not paid if members go outside the network.

Experience rating—A method of calculating health insurance premiums for a group based entirely or partly on the risks the group presents. An employer whose employees are unhealthy will pay higher rates than one whose employees are healthier.

Experimental procedures—Health care services or procedures that: (1) public and private health insurance plans believe are not widely accepted as effective by American health care professionals; or (2) have not been scientifically proven to be effective for a particular disease or condition.

Explanation of benefits (EOB)—Forms sent to patients that explain which procedures and services were given, how much they cost, how much is covered by insurance, and how much the patient must pay.

Extended care facility (ECF)—A hospital unit for treatment of inpatients who require convalescent, rehabilitative, or long-term skilled nursing care.

Extracontractual benefits—Health care benefits beyond what the member's actual policy covers, typically provided to reduce utilization of higher-expense services.

Faculty practice plan—A form of physician group practice organized around a teaching program. It may be a single group encompassing all the physicians providing services to patients at the teaching hospital and clinics, or it may be multiple groups drawn along specialty lines.

False Claims Act—A Civil War–era federal law provided for prosecution of fraud against the U.S. government. It was misused by the Department of Justice (DOJ) in 1997 and 1998 to make widespread claims of fraud against hospitals for Medicare billing errors, threatening immediate prosecution if settlement payments were not paid to the government. Under pressure, the DOJ later issued new False Claims Act guidelines that better differentiated billing errors from substantial evidence of intentional fraud and provided hospitals with relief.

Family practitioner/practice physician (FP)—A doctor who specializes in the care and treatment of all family members, including adults and children. These physicians can perform a wide range of services, including delivering babies, but usually do not perform surgeries. In many health care plans, family practice physicians serve as gatekeepers.

Favorable selection—The enrollment of a higher-than-average number of low-risk or relatively healthy members into a managed care organization. See also *Adverse selection.*

Favored nations' discount—A contractual agreement between a provider and a payer stating that the provider will automatically provide the payer the best discount it provides anyone else.

Federal acquisition regulations (FAR)—The regulations applied to the federal government's acquisition of services, including health care services.

Federal Employee Health Benefit Acquisition Regulations (FEHBARS)—The regulations applied to the federal Office of Personnel Management's purchase of health care benefits programs for federal employees.

Fee-for-service (FFS)—A traditional indemnity method of payment in which each service provided to patients is associated with a corresponding fee to be paid to the provider.

Fee schedule—A schedule of maximum dollar amounts that are payable to health care providers for certain services or procedures. Also known as a *fee allowance schedule,* it is usually based on CPT billing codes.

File and use—The submission of contracts or rates filed with a state's insurance commissioner and typically automatically usable by an insurance company within a specific period unless specifically rejected.

First-dollar coverage—A rapidly disappearing type of health insurance policy with no required deductible.

Fiscal intermediary (FI)—An entity, usually an insurance company, that has a contract with the HCFA to determine and make Medicare payments for Part A and certain Part B benefits to hospitals and other providers of services and to perform related functions.

501(c)(3)—The section of the U.S. tax code that defines not-for-profit, charitable, tax-exempt organizations.

Fixed costs—Costs, such as rent and utilities, that do not vary with the output or activity of an organization.

Flexible benefits—An employer-administered program allowing employees to select and trade between health care and other benefits based on their specific needs. Flexible benefits are permitted by section 125 of the IRS Code. Also called *cafeteria benefits.*

For-profit hospital—A hospital operated for the purpose of making a profit for its owner(s). The initial source of funding is typically through the sale of stock; profits are paid to shareholders in dividends. Also referred to as a *proprietary* or *investor-owned hospital.*

Foundation for Accountability (FACCT)—Established in 1995, a not-for-profit organization that works to evaluate the manner in which health plans treat individual medical conditions or diseases. FACCT creates tools that help people understand and use quality-of-care information, develops consumer-focused quality measures, and supports public education about health care quality.

Foundation model—The model for forming a hospital or health care system as a new tax-exempt corporation that acquires the tangible and intangible assets of a medical group and contracts with the medical group for professional services. The foundation employs all nonphysician staff and is responsible for management, facilities, equipment, and support services. The contracting medical group remains independent, with a board composed entirely of physicians.

Freestanding ambulatory care center—A health care facility that is physically separate from a hospital and provides health care on an outpatient basis. There are three types of centers: freestanding emergency center, freestanding urgent care center, and primary care center.

Freestanding ambulatory surgery center—A health care facility that is physically separate from a hospital and provides prescheduled surgical services on an out-patient basis, generally at a lower cost than inpatient hospital care. Also called a *freestanding outpatient surgery center* or *surgicenter.*

Freestanding emergency center (FEC)—A type of freestanding ambulatory care center that is designed, organized, equipped, and staffed to provide medical care for injuries and illnesses, including those that are life-threatening.

Freestanding facilities—Health care facilities that are not physically, administratively, or financially connected to a hospital. An example is a freestanding ambulatory surgery center.

Freestanding urgent care center—A type of freestanding ambulatory care center that provides primary and urgent care treatment on a less than 24-hour per day basis. The center is not equipped to treat medical emergencies and does not provide follow-up care.

Full-time-equivalent (FTE) personnel—Full-time employees; total FTE personnel is calculated by dividing the hospital's total number of paid hours by 2080, the number of annual paid hours for one full-time employee.

Gag clause—A provision within managed care contracts that would restrict communication between physician and patient.

Gatekeeper—A health care professional who coordinates, manages, and authorizes all health care services provided to a covered beneficiary. May be a nurse, social worker, physician's assistant, or a primary care physician (e.g., internist, family/general practitioner, pediatrician, and, in some cases, OB/GYN).

General practitioner—A doctor who practices general medicine and is involved in primary care.

Generics—Drugs that have the same chemical equivalents as a brand-name drug and are typically less expensive. Generic equivalents are often prescribed as a cost-saving alternative.

Global budget—A cost-containment strategy whereby providers and hospitals in a given system or service region receive fixed budgets for health care or must adhere to a statewide or nationwide limit on overall public and private spending for health care services.

Global capitation—A fixed prepayment per patient that covers all professional, institutional, and medical expenses; sometimes called *total capitation.*

Global fee—A payment mechanism that consists of a single fee for all aspects and services surrounding a hospital admission or an episode of care; i.e., a single payment for all professional, diagnostic, and facility-based services. Also referred to as a *package price.* See also **Bundled billing.**

Global payment—A payment arrangement in which hospitals and physicians share in one prospectively determined/negotiated, comprehensive fee for a specific service, such as heart surgery, often to achieve marketing advantages.

Governing body—The legal entity ultimately responsible for hospital policy, organization, management, and quality of care. The governing body is accountable to the owner(s) of the hospital, which may be a corporation, the community, local government, or shareholders. Also called the *governing board, board of trustees, commissioners,* or *directors.*

Graduate medical education (GME)—The period of medical training that follows graduation from medical school, commonly referred to as internship, residency, and fellowship training.

Grievance system—A formal complaint (verbal or written) system required by state and federal law for HMO members and providers to voice complaints, seek remedies, or request review of supplemental benefits.

Group contract—The legal description of a group's specific health care benefits and services covered by whom, where, and under what conditions, as well as limits to that coverage.

Grouper—A specific computer program that classifies patient bills by diagnosis-related group.

Group insurance—The most common type of health insurance in the United States. Over 75 percent of all health insurance is offered through businesses, union trusts, or other groups and associations. For insurance purposes, most groups are composed of full-time employees.

Group-model HMO—An HMO that contracts with one or more multispecialty groups to provide services to beneficiaries. The contracting group receives either a capitated payment or a percentage of the HMO's premium in exchange for providing both primary and specialty care services to persons enrolled in the HMO. Compensation and distributions to the physicians practicing within the medical group are left to the discretion of the medical group itself. See also *Capitation; Health maintenance organization (HMO); Independent practice association (IPA) model HMO; Staff model HMO.*

Group practice—The provision of medical services by three or more physicians formally organized to provide medical care, consultation, diagnosis, and/or treatment through the joint use of equipment and personnel. The income from the medical practice is distributed in accordance with methods determined by members of the group. Group practices have a single-specialty or multispecialty focus.

Group practice without walls (GPWW)—A legal organization that consists of a network of physicians who maintain their own private practices. The GPWW purchases the assets of each practice, but physicians keep autonomy by seeing private patients, keeping their own employees, and making their own schedules. Also referred to as a *clinic without walls.*

HCFA 1500—A claims form required by Medicare but also used by many private insurance companies and managed care plans to bill for services.

HCFA Common Procedural Coding System (HCPCS)—A set of codes used within the Medicare system to describe and define health care services and procedures. The HCPCS includes CPT-4 (Current Procedural Terminology, 4th Revision) codes in addition to codes for nonprocedures, such as durable medical equipment and ambulance transportation.

Health alliance—A large conglomerate of businesses and consumers formed to negotiate prices for health benefits with HMOs or networks of physicians, hospitals, insurers, and other health care providers. See also *Health insurance purchasing cooperative (HIPC)*.

Health and Human Services (HHS)—The U.S. Department of Health and Human Services, formerly the Department of Health, Education and Welfare.

Health Care Financing Administration (HCFA)—The federal agency that administers the Medicare and Medicaid programs and determines provider certification and reimbursement.

Health care reform—Changes to the overall health care delivery system: its structure, financing, coverage, and services.

Health care system—A corporate body that owns, leases, and/or manages multiple entities, including hospitals, long-term care facilities, other institutional providers and programs, physician practices, and/or insurance functions.

Health Insurance Portability and Accountability Act of 1996 (HIPAA)—A federal law that made many changes in employer-sponsored health plans. The law allows individuals to move from job to job without losing coverage as the result of preexisting conditions. HIPAA also guarantees access to group coverage for employees in companies with 2 to 50 employees.

Health insurance purchasing cooperative (HIPC)—A concept included in the Clinton health care reform proposal and in managed competition policies for correcting the failures of the small group insurance market. In theory, these cooperatives would pool the resources of individual businesses and groups into larger pools, thus spreading the insurance risks and increasing the health care purchasing power across the aggregate of HIPC members.

Health maintenance organization (HMO)—A prepaid health plan that acts as both an insurer and a provider of comprehensive health services. HMO subscribers pay a capitated fee and are limited to the hospitals and physicians affiliated with the HMO. See also *Capitation; Independent practice association (IPA) model HMO; Group model HMO; Managed care; Staff model HMO.*

Health plan—A network of doctors, hospitals, and insurers that provides coverage through contracts negotiated with health alliances.

Health Plan Employer Data and Information Set (HEDIS)—A data-reporting system developed by the NCQA focusing on quality, access, patient satisfaction, membership, utilization, and finances.

Health promotion—The process of fostering awareness, influencing attitudes, and identifying alternatives so that individuals can make informed choices and change their behavior in order to achieve an optimum level of physical and mental health.

High-risk insurance pool—A special insurance pool in some states from which people with a chronic disease or illness, such as diabetes or multiple sclerosis, can purchase health care insurance. These funds are for people who can afford to pay the insurance premiums, which are high, but who would not be eligible elsewhere because of their disease or disability. Additional funds for these high-risk pools are typically derived from health insurance premium taxes.

Hill-Burton program—A federal program of financial assistance created by the Hospital Survey and Construction Act of 1946 for the construction and modernization of health care facilities. In return for this funding, hospitals are required to provide a specified level of charity care each year.

Hold harmless clause—A contractual clause whereby the provider agrees not to sue or make any claims against a plan member for covered services even if the plan becomes insolvent or fails to meet its financial obligations. This clause is found in many managed care contracts between payers and providers and is required by many states.

Holding company—A separate entity used to hold a variety of subsidiary groups that often perform related functions but have a distinct corporate identity.

Holistic health—Health viewed from the perspective that the patient is collectively more than the sum of his or her parts; that body, mind, and spirit must be in harmony to achieve optimum health, and, therefore, that a multidisciplinary approach to health care is required.

Home and community-based waiver (HCFA 2176 waiver)—A waiver allowing states to offer an alternative set of health care benefits for people who would otherwise require long-term nursing care in an intermediate care facility for persons with mental retardation (ICF/MR) or hospital care. Services under the waiver may include respite care, adaptive equipment, case management, homemaker services, personal care, private duty nursing, and more.

Home health care—Health care service provided in a patient's home rather than a hospital or other institutional setting. The services include nursing care; social services; and physical, speech, or occupational therapy.

Horizontal integration—The linkage or network of similar types of providers, often in different geographic regions and serving different markets. It is used as a competitive strategy by some hospitals to control the geographic distribution of health care services.

Hospice—The provision of medical care and support services (such as pain and symptom management, counseling, and bereavement services) to terminally ill patients and their families. A hospice may be a freestanding facility, a unit of a hospital or other institution, or a separate program of a hospital, agency, or institution that assists the patient at home.

Hospital—A health care institution with an organized medical and professional staff and with inpatient beds available around the clock. Its primary function is to provide inpatient medical, nursing, and other health-related services to patients for both surgical and nonsurgical conditions. It also typically provides some outpatient services, particularly emergency care. Each state has its own definition of hospital for licensure purposes.

Hospital affiliation—(1) An association established by a contractual agreement between a health plan and one or more hospitals to provide the inpatient benefits offered by a health plan. (2) An arrangement between hospitals and other health care financing or provider organizations.

Hospital alliance—An association established by an agreement among hospitals to voluntarily join together on some services to reduce costs and achieve economies of scale.

Hospital market basket—Components of the overall cost of hospital care.

Hospital market basket index (HMBI)—A measure of inflation of the cost of goods and services purchased by hospitals.

Hospital-physician alliance (HPA)—A partnership between a hospital and a group of its staff physicians. Such alliances range from an informal sharing of expertise to a more structured arrangement involving computer networking, assistance with physician recruitment, and physician practice development. Examples of formal HPA structures include: physician-hospital organizations for managed care contracting, management service organizations for practice management, and integrated delivery systems for development of a broad range of clinical services.

Hospital preauthorization—A managed care technique requiring the insured to obtain permission from a managed care organization before entering the hospital for nonemergency care.

Hospital-surgical policy—A type of health insurance policy that pays specific benefits for hospital services, including room and board and surgery.

House staff—An aggregate body of physicians and dentists in training who participate in an accredited program of graduate medical education sponsored by a hospital.

Hybrid HMO—A type of HMO that combines characteristics of more than one of the four principal HMO models. Hybrid HMOs may include features of indemnity insurance, such as coinsurance, deductibles, experience rating, and an open panel of providers in addition to basic HMO utilization, cost, and access controls. See also *Mixed model managed care plan.*

Incentives—Financial rewards built into the health care system to encourage providers or patients to act in a certain way. The doctor's financial incentive in the fee-for-service system is to perform more procedures or services because pay is based on services rendered. In a managed care system with fixed fees, usually paid in advance, the incentive is to do fewer procedures, use fewer specialists, and keep the patient well.

Incidence—The number of new cases of a disease or condition in a defined population within a specific period.

Incurred but not reported (IBNR)—An accounting term that means health care services have been provided but the bill has not yet reached the insurer. It allows calculating an insurer's liability and reserve needs. Incurred claims are the legal obligation an insurer has for services that have been provided during a specific period.

Indemnity carrier—Usually an insurance company or benevolent association that offers selected insurance coverage within a framework of fee schedules, limitations, and exclusions as negotiated with subscriber groups. Reimbursement is applied after the third-party carrier reviews and processes filed claims. Aetna, CIGNA, and Prudential are examples of indemnity carriers.

Indemnity insurance—Coverage offered by insurance companies in which insured individuals are reimbursed for the medical expenses they incur or payment is made directly to providers for these expenses.

Independent practice association (IPA) model HMO—An HMO model under which independent doctors and/or small group practices contract with an HMO to provide services to an enrolled population. The physicians may own the HMO and are usually reimbursed on a fee-for-service basis with a percentage withheld. This "pool" of funds held by the IPA's administration can be redistributed to the doctors in a profitable year. See also *Capitation; Group model HMO; Health maintenance organization (HMO); Managed care; Staff model HMO.*

Indian Health Services (IHS)—A division of the U.S. Public Health Service that is responsible for providing federal health services for American Indians and Alaska natives.

Indigent care—Medical care for those who cannot afford it. See also *Medically indigent; Uncompensated care.*

Indirect medical education (IME) adjustment—A Medicare payment adjustment applied to DRG and outlier payments under prospective payment for hospitals that operate an approved graduate medical education program. It is based on the hospital's ratio of interns and residents to average daily occupancy.

Individual case management—The determination by utilization management professionals of individual patients' care (usually high-cost, high-resource intensive care) in order to find the most appropriate and cost-effective course of treatment, even if it involves paying for services not routinely covered by the health plan.

Injury independent of all other means—An injury resulting from an accident, provided that the accident was not caused by an illness.

Inpatient—A patient receiving acute care through admission to the hospital for a stay of longer than 24 hours.

Integrated delivery system (IDS)—A regional health care network or system providing a broad range of services (a continuum of care from acute care and outpatient ambulatory care to skilled nursing and long-term care) to a defined patient population within a certain geographical area.

Integrated health care organization (IHO)—An integrated delivery system that is predominantly owned by physicians.

Integrated provider (IP)—A group that provides comprehensive and coordinated care, typically including hospitals, group practices, a health plan, and other related health care services. Physicians may either be employees of the IP or have their own practice.

Intensity of services—The quantity and quality of resources used in producing a patient care service, such as a hospital admission or home health visit. Intensity of services reflects, for example, the amount of nursing care, diagnostic procedures, and supplies furnished.

Intensive care unit (ICU)—A hospital unit for treatment and continuous monitoring of inpatients with life-threatening conditions. See also *Step-down unit.*

Intermediate care facility (ICF)—A facility that provides nursing, supervisory, and supportive services to elderly or chronically ill patients who do not require the degree of care or treatment that a skilled nursing unit is designed to provide.

Internal medicine physicians (internists)—Primary care physicians primarily for adults. Unlike family practice physicians, they normally do not care for children and may perform surgeries.

International Classification of Diseases, 10th Revision, Clinical Modification (ICD-10-CM)—The latest version of a diagnosis and procedure classification system designed to facilitate the collection of uniform and comparable health information. This system is used to group patients into primary, secondary, and other diagnoses for claims reporting.

Investor-owned hospital—See also *For-profit hospital.*

Job-lock—A situation in which people cannot leave their jobs without losing insurance coverage for themselves or for family members who have an existing illness or condition.

Joint Commission on Accreditation of Healthcare Organizations (JCAHO)—An independent, voluntary, not-for-profit accreditation body sponsored by the American College of Physicians, the American College of Surgeons, the American Hospital Association, the American Medical Association, and the American Dental Association. The JCAHO conducts accreditation surveys for hospitals and other health care organizations.

Joint conference committee (JCC)—A hospital committee composed of governing board, administration, and medical staff members whose purpose is to facilitate communication among these groups.

Joint venture—A cooperative financial relation between two parties (i.e., hospital and physician group, two hospitals, hospital and HMO) in which each shares risks and benefits.

Large claim pooling—A means of helping small groups keep their insurance premiums from sudden increases if they have a costly case or claim. All groups with one insurer contribute funds to a large pool; and claims over a specific amount per individual are charged to the large claim pool rather than to the funds for expected claims. By separating large claims from the company's expected claims, companies are able, up to a point, to keep their premiums from fluctuating.

Legend drug—A medication that cannot be given without a prescription.

Length of stay (LOS)—The number of calendar days that elapse between an inpatient's admission and discharge.

Level playing field—A goal of having all insurers governed by the same rules and regulations. ERISA employers are not subject to state law that governs commercial and not-for-profit insurers and Blue Cross and Blue Shield. Blue Cross and Blue Shield plans are taxed differently for premiums than are commercial insurers. Health care benefit deductions for employers and employees also differ between corporations and small businesses, according to IRS rules.

Leverage—See *Capital structure.*

Licensed facilities—Health care sites that require licenses by the state or federal government to offer health care services.

Licensed practical nurse (LPN)—A nurse who has completed a practical nursing education program and is licensed by a state to provide routine care under the direction of a registered nurse or physician. Referred to as a *licensed vocational nurse (LVN)* in California and Texas.

Licensure—A formal process by which a government agency grants an individual the legal right to practice an occupation; grants an organization the legal right to engage in an activity, such as operation of a hospital; and prohibits all other individuals and organizations from legally doing so, to ensure that the public health, safety, and welfare are reasonably well protected.

Life care—Long-term, continuing care offered by retirement communities to their residents on a contract basis through provision of services ranging from independent living to skilled nursing home care.

Life safety code—A standard developed and updated by the National Fire Protection Association that specifies construction and operational conditions to minimize fire hazards and provide a system of safety in case of fire.

Lifetime reserve—The lifetime pool of 60 days of inpatient hospitalization benefits that may be drawn upon by a patient when he or she has exhausted the maximum benefit allowed under Medicare for a single bout of illness.

Liquidity—Financial ratios that measure the ability of a corporation to meet its short-term liabilities as they come due.

Living will—A document through which a person can indicate his or her preference not to receive "heroic" or "extraordinary" treatments to support or prolong life.

Lock-in—A term used to describe the situation of members in a health plan, such as an HMO, who must use only those doctors, hospitals, or other facilities that are in the plan. Any care given by a nonplan provider will usually not be covered by the plan, unless it is an emergency.

Long-term care (LTC)—Services designed to provide diagnostic, preventive, therapeutic, rehabilitative, supportive, and maintenance care and oversight for individuals who have chronic physical and/or mental impairments (and assist their informal caregivers); this care is provided in a variety of settings, including the home, specialty facilities, and nursing homes.

Loss ratio—A measure of a health plan's financial well-being that examines the difference between its expenditures on paid claims, incurred claims, and administrative expenses and its revenue from individual premiums.

Magnetic resonance—See *Nuclear magnetic resonance imaging.*

Major teaching hospitals—Hospitals defined by Medicare as having an approved graduate medical education program and a ratio of interns and residents to beds of .25 or greater for purposes of making additional payments under Medicare's indirect medical education adjustment.

Malpractice—The act of providing health care services without exercising the degree of skill and care generally exercised by like professionals under similar circumstances.

Managed care—Any system of health service payment or delivery arrangements in which the health plan attempts to control or coordinate the use of health services by its enrolled members to contain health expenditures, improve quality, or both. Often involves a defined delivery system of providers with some form of contractual arrangement with the plan. See also *Health maintenance organization (HMO), Independent practice association (IPA) model HMO,* and *Preferred provider organization (PPO).*

Managed care network—A regional or national organization of providers owned by a commercial insurance company or other sponsor (e.g., a managed care plan) and offered to employers and other groups or organizations as either an alternative to, or a total replacement for, traditional indemnity health insurance.

Managed care organization (MCO)—A plan or a company, such as an HMO, PPO, or exclusive provider organization (EPO), that uses the principles of managed care as a basic part of doing business. See also *Managed care plan (MCP).*

Managed care plan (MCP)—A type of group health plan designed to provide necessary, appropriate, efficient, and cost-effective health services to enrollees through contractual arrangements with chosen providers. MCPs typically include financial incentives for enrollees to use providers associated with the plan as well as formal programs of quality assurance and utilization review. See also **Managed care organization (MCO).**

Managed choice—A type of managed care plan that combines elements of managed care, such as restricted provider choice and traditional indemnity insurance, with no restrictions on provider selection.

Managed competition—An economic theory/mechanism designed to blend government regulation with competition in the marketplace and under which employers join large purchasing cooperatives to buy health care services from a network of providers in order to compete for consumers based on price, quality, and a standardized package of benefits.

Managed indemnity plan (MIP)—An indemnity health insurance plan that incorporates certain managed care procedures, such as a required second surgical opinion, preadmission certification, and concurrent utilization review, to control costs and ensure the quality of provided services. MIPs offer members the same latitude in choosing providers as traditional fee-for-service insurance. Also called *managed fee-for-service insurance.*

Management information system (MIS)—The computer hardware and software that provide the support for managing a health plan or delivery system, including all data information collection processes and the utilization of collected data elements.

Management service organization (MSO)—An organization that provides administrative and practice management services to medical groups, which are typically owned by physicians; it is usually a subsidiary of the group. It owns all business assets, but the clinic assets stay with the medical group.

Mandated benefits—Coverage that states require insurers to include in health insurance policies, such as prenatal care, mammographic screening, and care for newborns. Sometimes called *state mandates.*

Mandated providers—The range of health care providers required by federal or state law to be included in any health plan.

Mandatory enrollment—A requirement under individual state Medicaid programs stipulating that all recipients or certain categories of recipients enroll in a managed care program. States must request and receive a waiver from the HCFA to initiate such a requirement.

Marginal cost—The cost of producing an extra unit of product; a key consideration in pricing and in calculating cost implications of business expansion or contraction.

Market basket index—An index of the annual change in the prices of goods and services that providers use for producing health services. There are separate market baskets for Medicare's prospective payment system's (PPS's) hospital operating and capital inputs; PPS-excluded facility operating inputs; and SNF, home health agency, and renal dialysis facility operating and capital inputs.

Market-driven health reform—Renovations in the general health care system, in both financing and delivery of services, that emanate from the private sector and are associated with managed care principles in which health provider organizations and networks compete on the basis of cost, quality, and access to care. Thus, the strategy is based on marketplace dynamics of competition and price rather than government regulation, management, or rate setting.

Marketing—Activities making information about a health organization or plan known to consumers or eligible persons for the purpose of persuading them to utilize the organization or enroll with the plan.

Market share—In the context of managed care, that part of the market potential that a health care organization or a managed care company has captured or wishes to penetrate. Market share is usually expressed as a percentage of the market potential, for instance, the percentage of a market's population that is enrolled in a managed care company's plan.

Master group contract—The actual contract between a health plan and a group that purchases coverage, setting out specific terms of coverage, rights, and responsibilities of both parties.

Maximum allowable costs (MACs)—A list that health plans distribute to their participating pharmacies describing the maximum amount the plan will pay for specific medications.

Maximum out-of-pocket costs—The maximum a plan member will have to pay from his or her own funds for deductibles, copayments, or other expenses during the contract period.

Means test—An annual income and assets test to determine if a person or family has an income that qualifies for public support, such as Medicaid.

Medicaid—A joint federal-state program that, since 1966, has paid much of the health care costs of certain (but not all) low-income persons. The federal government sets certain minimum rules and payment levels and provides some of the funding, and each state administers the program, contributes additional funds, and may establish additional eligibility rules and benefits.

Medical care evaluation studies—An organized collection of concurrent or retrospective information about important aspects of patient care provided by the medical staff to assess clinical competence and identify and correct patient care problems.

Medical center—A hospital or hospitals affiliated with a medical school that provide a broad range of medical and health-related services to patients.

Medical foundation—A tax-exempt medical group practice conducting research and offering educational programs.

Medical group—An organized collection of physicians who have a common business interest through a partnership or some form of shared ownership. Some medical groups consist of a group of physicians representing a single specialty; other groups are made up of physicians from two or more specialties.

Medical loss ratio—The ratio between the cost to deliver medical care and the amount of money that a plan receives. Insurance companies often have a medical loss ratio of 92 percent or more; tightly managed HMOs may have medical loss ratios of 75 percent to 85 percent, although the overhead (or administrative cost ratio) is concomitantly higher. The medical loss ratio is dependent on the amount of money brought in as well as the cost of delivering care; thus, if the rates are too low, the ratio may be high even though the actual cost of delivering care is not out of line.

Medically indigent—People who do not have public or private insurance coverage. See also *Indigent care.*

Medically necessary—Term used to describe covered services required to preserve and maintain the health status of a member or eligible person in accordance with the standards of medical practice in the medical community where services are rendered.

Medically underserved area—A geographic location that has insufficient health resources to meet the medical needs of the resident population.

Medical policy—The policy of a health plan regarding what will be paid for as medical benefits.

Medical record—A written or electronic account of a person's medical history, current illness, diagnosis, details of treatments, and chronological notes on the progress a patient makes toward healing or recovery. Each patient is entitled to read his or her medical record, authenticated by the signature of his or her physician. The medical record must be legible, and there are strict rules regarding the confidentiality of the personal information it contains.

Medical savings account (MSA)—A health insurance option consisting of a high-deductible insurance policy and tax-advantaged savings account. Individuals pay for their own health care up to the annual deductible by withdrawing from the savings account or paying out of pocket. The insurance policy pays for most or all costs of covered services once the deductible is met. Also called *personal health accounts.*

Medical staff–hospital organization (MeSH)—See *Physician-hospital organization (PHO).*

Medicare—The federal health insurance program for people age 65 and over and those with certain chronic disabilities. Medicare has two parts: Part A (hospital insurance) pays for most inpatient hospital care and some follow-up care; Part B (medical insurance) pays for most physicians' services. Patients are responsible for deductibles and copayments. Medicare pays hospitals for patient care using a prospective pricing system based on diagnosis-related groups.

Medicare+Choice—A program created by the Balanced Budget Act of 1997 to replace the existing system of Medicare risk and cost contracts. Beneficiaries have the choice during an open season each year to enroll in a Medicare+Choice plan or to remain in traditional Medicare. Medicare+Choice plans may include coordinated care plans (HMOs, PPOs, or plans offered by provider-sponsored organizations);

private fee-for-service plans; or high-deductible plans with medical savings accounts.

Medicare cost report—An annual report required of institutions participating in the Medicare program that records each institution's total costs and charges associated with providing services to all patients, the portion of those costs and charges allocated to Medicare patients, and the Medicare payments received.

Medicare fee schedule—The resource-based fee schedule Medicare uses to pay for physicians' services.

Medicare Part A—The hospital insurance portion of Medicare that pays for inpatient hospital care.

Medicare Part B—The medical insurance portion of Medicare that pays for outpatient and physician services that are not covered under Part A.

Medicare Payment Advisory Commission (MedPAC)—An advisory body of independent experts created by the U.S. Congress to provide guidance on Medicare provider payment issues. The former Prospective Payment Assessment Commission (ProPAC) and Physician Payment Review Commission (PPRC) were merged into the MedPAC at its creation in 1997.

Medicare risk contract—A contract between Medicare and a health plan under which the plan receives monthly capitated payments to provide Medicare-covered services for enrollees and thereby assumes insurance risk for those enrollees. A plan is eligible for a risk contract if it is a federally qualified HMO or a competitive medical plan. To be phased out during the transition to the Medicare+Choice program.

Medicare-supplement policy—See *Medigap coverage* or *insurance.*

Medigap coverage or **insurance**—Privately purchased individual or group health insurance policies designed to supplement Medicare coverage. Benefits may include payment of Medicare deductibles, coinsurance, and balance bills as well as payment for services not covered by Medicare. Medigap insurance must conform to one of 10 federally standardized benefit packages.

Member—An individual who has enrolled in a health care plan as a subscriber or a dependent of a subscriber for whom the plan has accepted the responsibility for providing health services as specified in the health plan contract. Sometimes called an *enrollee.* See also *Subscriber.*

Member months—The unit of volume measurement used by managed care plans to count the total number of months of coverage for each plan member. Each member month is the equivalent of one member for whom the managed care plan is paid one month's premium. Member months accumulate for year-to-date statistical purposes.

Mental Health Parity Act—A 1995 federal law requiring that a plan may not establish a dollar limit on mental health benefits as long as the plan does not impose such limits on medical and surgical benefits. If a plan decides to impose an annual limit on medical and surgical benefits, then the limits for mental health benefits must be of equal value.

Merger—The union of two or more organizations by the transfer of all assets to one organization that continues to exist while the other(s) is (are) dissolved.

Messenger model—A managed care negotiation model used to avoid antitrust restrictions. Consists of negotiating fee-for-service contracts between numerous providers and a managed care organization through use of an independent messenger, who negotiates with each provider individually for a fee acceptable to both the payer and the provider. Under the messenger model, providers are not permitted to discuss among themselves any payment information.

Midlevel practitioner (MLP)—Nurses, physician assistants, midwives, and other nonphysicians who can deliver medical care under the sponsorship of a practicing physician.

Military treatment facilities—Hospitals and other health care clinics that are managed by one of the uniformed services within the Department of Defense, such as the Air Force or Navy.

Minor emergency facility—See *Urgent care center.*

Mission statement—A written expression that sets forth the purpose of an organization and usually precedes the development of goals and objectives.

Mixed model managed care plan—A type of managed care plan that uses two or more modes of service delivery. For example, a mixed model HMO may own and operate a staff model in which the physicians are employees of the HMO; and the HMO may also contract with an IPA, which has individual physicians with private practices. See also *Hybrid HMO.*

Model HMO Act—Developed by the National Association of Insurance Commissioners to guide states' development of their own HMO acts, it has been implemented partially or completely by many states. It requires HMOs to meet certain financial requirements, effectively provide basic health care services to enrollees on a prepaid basis, and ensure that these services are rendered under reasonable standards of care consistent with prevailing professionally recognized standards of medical practice.

Modified community rating—A technique that bases premium costs on the health-risk rating in a particular geographic area, accounting for health status, age, and sex differences within the community.

Morbidity—The incidence of illness, injury, or disability in a defined population.

Mortality—The incidence of death in a defined population.

Multidisciplinary team—An approach to caring for the elderly that involves a multidisciplinary team of professionals with the goal of providing comprehensive, integrated care. The team often includes a physician, nurse, and social worker working closely together and, depending on the patient's needs, may also include an occupational, physical, or other therapist and a psychiatrist or psychologist.

Multihospital system—Two or more hospitals owned, leased, contract managed, or sponsored by a central organization.

Multiple employer trust (MET)—A trust through which group health insurance policies are offered by an insurance benefit organization to employees and dependents of multiple employers. METs are regulated by some states.

Multiple employer welfare association (MEWA)—A group of employers that band together to purchase group health insurance for their employees. MEWAs are usually governed by ERISA, and individual state insurance laws do little to regulate them.

Multispecialty group (MSG)—A physician practice environment where diverse fields or specialties of medicine may converge to bring patients and purchasers a more unified and comprehensive service package.

National Association of Insurance Commissioners (NAIC)—The national group of state officials who regulate insurance practices in each of the states.

National Committee for Quality Assurance (NCQA)—A national organization that conducts quality-focused reviews of HMOs and other managed care plans. NCQA is in the process of developing a "report card" to measure quality of care at HMOs.

National Drug Code (NDC)—The identifying number for medicines maintained by the Food and Drug Administration (FDA).

National Practitioner Data Bank (NPDB)—A national databank that contains information concerning claims and disciplinary actions filed against physicians and other medical practitioners.

Neonatal—The part of an infant's life from the hour of birth through the first 27 days, 23 hours and 59 minutes; the infant is referred to as a *newborn* throughout this period.

Net loss ratio—A measure of a plan's financial stability, derived by dividing its medical costs and other expenses by its income from premiums.

Network—A group of providers, typically linked through contractual arrangements, that provide a defined set of benefits.

Network model HMO—An HMO that contracts with several different medical groups, often at a capitated rate. Groups may use different methods to pay their physicians.

Nonparticipating physician or **provider**—A physician or other provider who does not sign a participation agreement and, therefore, is not obligated to accept assignment on all Medicare claims, or those who have not contracted with or are not employed by a health plan to deliver services to its members. The latter are also called *non-network providers* or *out-of-network providers*. See also **Assignment; Participating physician** or **provider.**

Nonprice competition—Competition between two products or services based on factors other than price; for example, quality, convenience, or packaging.

Nosocomial infection—An infection that may be measured by its rate of frequency of occurrence and that is acquired by an individual while receiving care or services in a health care organization.

Not-for-profit hospital—A hospital that operates on a not-for-profit basis under the ownership of a private corporation. Typically, a not-for-profit hospital is run by a board of trustees, is exempt from federal and state taxes, and uses its profits to cover capital expenses and future operating costs.

Nuclear magnetic resonance (NMR) imaging—A diagnostic tool using visualization of cross-sectional images of body tissue and strong static magnetic and radio-frequency fields to monitor body chemistry noninvasively.

Nuclear medicine—The use of radioisotopes to study and treat disease, especially in the diagnostic area.

Nurse—A person qualified by a formal training program at an accredited school of nursing and licensed by the state to practice nursing services to patients requiring assistance.

Nurse clinician—A registered nurse qualified by advanced training in a nursing specialty who practices, teaches, consults, supervises, or coordinates nursing services in that specialty.

Nurse practitioner (NP) A licensed nurse who has completed a nurse practitioner program at the master's or certificate level and is trained in providing primary care services; expanded health care evaluations and decision making; and diagnosis, treatment, and prescriptions under a physician's supervision.

Nursing home A health facility with inpatient beds and an organized professional staff that provides continuous nursing and other health-related, psychosocial, and personal services to patients who are not in an acute phase of illness but who primarily require continued care on an inpatient basis.

Occupancy—The inpatient census, generally expressed as a percentage of total beds that are occupied at any given time.

Occupational Safety and Health Administration (OSHA)—An agency of the U.S. Department of Labor charged with the responsibility of reducing occupational exposure and risk to workers' health and safety. OSHA establishes rules, monitors compliance through inspection, and enforces rules through penalties and fines for noncompliant organizations.

Occurrence—An incident that requires the rendering of health care services covered by a contract with an HMO or other prepaid health care plan. An occurrence includes admission to a hospital, a physician visit, emergency treatment, or a similar event.

Occurrence coverage—Once the most common type of commercial malpractice insurance, coverage for liability arising from malpractice that occurred while the policy was in effect, regardless of when the claim or potential loss is reported.

Office of Managed Care (OMC)—The federal agency in the HCFA responsible for overseeing federal qualification and compliance issues for HMOs.

Open access—A managed care model allowing patients direct access to a specialist without first receiving a referral from either a gatekeeper or primary care physician.

Open-ended or **open-access HMO**—An HMO that allows its members to seek care from other than staff or participating providers at an additional cost. See also *Point-of-service (POS) plan.*

Open enrollment period—Time during which uninsured individuals may join a health care plan or insured individuals can switch plans without demonstrating their health status. See also *Enrollment.*

Open-panel HMO—An HMO that allows any willing provider to contract with it, providing that the provider meets all the requirements set forth by the HMO.

Open staff—As applied to the medical staff as a whole, an agreement under which physicians provide administrative and clinical services to a hospital on a nonexclusive basis. See also *Closed panel.*

Opportunity cost—The cost of a lost opportunity; that is, the value given up by using a resource in one way instead of in an alternative, better way.

Outcomes—The end results of health care that are usually measured in terms of cost, mortality, health status, and quality of life or patient function. Outcome measures are the specific criteria used to determine or describe the outcome.

Outcomes measurement—The process of systematically tracking a patient's clinical treatment and responses to that treatment using generally accepted outcome measures or quality indicators.

Outcomes research—A specialized branch of health services investigation designed to determine the relative effectiveness of specific treatments for specific health conditions.

Outliers—Cases that are substantially different from the rest of the population. With regard to hospital payment, these are classified as cases with extremely long lengths of stay (day outliers) or extraordinarily high costs (cost outliers) compared with others in the same DRG. Hospitals receive additional PPS payments for these cases.

Out of area—A place where the plan will not pay for services or benefits. Out of area can refer to a geographical location as well as to benefits or services outside a specific group of providers.

Out-of-network services—Health care services received by a plan member from a noncontracted provider. Reimbursement is usually lower when a member goes out of the network, and other financial penalties may apply.

Out-of-pocket expenditures—Health-related expenditures for which beneficiaries are financially liable. For Medicare beneficiaries, the total amount includes cost sharing for Medicare-covered services (for example, deductibles, copayments, and balance bills); the cost of Medicare Part B and private health insurance premiums; and the cost of noncovered services. See also *Balance billing; Coinsurance; Copayment; Cost sharing; Deductible.*

Out-of-pocket limit—The total amount of money, including deductibles, copayments, and coinsurance, as defined in the contract, that plan members must pay out of their own pockets toward eligible expenses for themselves and/or dependents.

Out-of-pocket payments (OOP)—Cash payments made by a plan member or insured person to the provider in the form of deductibles, coinsurance, or copayments during a defined period (usually a calendar year) before the out-of-pocket limit is reached.

Outpatient (OP)—A person who receives care without being admitted to the hospital for an overnight or longer stay.

Over-the-counter (OTC) drugs—Medications that may be obtained without a prescription.

Package price—See *Bundled billing; Global fee.*

Paid claims—The funds that health insurance plans pay to providers for approved services rendered. They do not include the patient's portion of those services, such as copayments. Paid claims are only those costs for which the plan is responsible according to the contract between the provider and the plan.

Paid claims loss ratio—The ratio of paid claims to premiums as a measure of a health plan's financial performance.

Par provider—A shorthand term for a participating professional or institutional provider who has signed an agreement with a plan to provide services.

Partial capitation—A payment per person per month for something less than the full range of covered services. This method is often used for primary care services.

Partial hospitalization services—Hospital programs that do not necessarily require inpatient care, such as substance abuse programs.

Participating physician or provider—A physician or other provider who signs a Medicare participation agreement, agreeing to accept assignment on all Medicare claims for one year, or those who are under contract with a health plan to provide services. See also *Nonparticipating physician* or *provider.*

PAS norms—The common term for Professional Activity Study results of the Commission on Professional and Hospital Activities (CPHA).

Patient advocate—See *Patient representative.*

Patient care committee—A hospital committee composed of medical, nursing, and other professional staff members whose purpose is to monitor all patient care practices and ensure that predetermined standards are met.

Patient care team—A multidisciplinary team organized under the leadership of a physician, with each member of the team having specific responsibilities and the entire team contributing to the care of the patient.

Patient compensation fund—A fund established by state law, most commonly financed by placing a surcharge on malpractice premiums of all professional liability policyholders in the state and used to pay malpractice claims.

Patient days—Each calendar day of care provided to a hospital inpatient under the terms of the patient's health plan excluding the day of discharge. "Patient days" is a measure of institutional use and is usually stated as the accumulated total number of inpatients (excluding newborns) each day for a given reporting period, tallied at a specified time (e.g., midnight) per 1,000 use rate, or patient days/1,000. Patient days are calculated by multiplying admissions by average length of stay.

Patient dumping—The refusal to examine, treat, and stabilize any person irrespective of payer/class who has an emergency medical condition or is in active labor or contractions once that person has been presented at a hospital emergency room or emergency department.

Patient mix—The numbers and types of patients served by a hospital or health program, classified according to their home, socioeconomic characteristics, diagnosis, or severity of illness. See also *Case mix.*

Patient ombudsman—See *Patient representative.*

Patient representative—A person who investigates and mediates patients' problems and complaints in relation to a hospital's services or health plan's coverage. Also called a *patient advocate* or *patient ombudsman.*

Patient satisfaction survey—A questionnaire used to solicit the perceptions of patients or plan enrollees regarding how a facility or health plan meets their medical needs and how the delivery of care is handled (e.g., waiting time and access to treatments).

Pay and pursue—The term applied to the practice whereby a plan pays a benefit first and then pursues another source of payment (e.g., another plan). Also called *pay and chase.*

Payer (payor)—Any agency, insurer, or health plan that pays for health care services and is responsible for the costs of those services.

Pediatricians—Doctors who specialize in the health care of infants and children and are considered primary care doctors for children.

Peer review—An evaluation conducted by practicing physicians or other clinical professionals of the appropriateness, effectiveness, and efficiency of medical services ordered or performed by other practicing physicians or clinical professionals.

Peer review organization (PRO)—An organization composed of physicians operating independently of the hospital and under contract with the federal government to determine whether care and service provided are medically necessary and meet professional standards under the Medicare and Medicaid programs. Also called *professional review organization.*

Percentage of premium—A payment mechanism that gives a provider a negotiated percentage of the monthly premium a payer receives for a specific benefits plan.

Per diem cost—Hospital or other inpatient institutional cost per day or for a day of care. Hospitals occasionally charge for their services on the basis of a per diem rate derived by dividing their total costs by the number of inpatient days of care given.

Per diem payment—Fixed daily payment that does not vary with the level of services used by the patient.

Performance measure—A quantitative tool (e.g., rate, ratio, index, percentage, and so on) that indicates an organization's performance in relation to a specified process or outcome. This can be a comparative indicator such as a benchmark.

Perinatal—The care of a woman after conception, of the woman and her fetus through pregnancy, and of the mother and her neonate until 28 days after childbirth.

Per member per month (PMPM)—The amount of money a health plan or provider receives per person every month. It is a way of calculating income and levels of payment. Also called *per subscriber per month (PSPM)* or *per contract per month (PCPM).*

Per member per year (PMPY)—The same unit of measurement as PMPM except that the period measured is one year.

Personal health account—See *Medical savings account (MSA).*

Per thousand members per year—A method used by managed care plans for reporting utilization of health services by plan members. Hospital utilization is usually expressed as days per thousand members per year.

Pharmacy benefit management (PBM) company—A large pharmaceutical marketing enterprise that focuses on purchasing pharmaceuticals at reduced prices from manufacturers and offering them at discounted prices to large employer health plans and hospitals.

Physician's assistant (PA)—A specially trained and licensed health professional who, under the supervision of a physician, performs certain medical procedures previously reserved to a physician.

Physician-assisted suicide—A phrase for euthanasia made visible by the actions of Dr. Jack Kevorkian. If legalized, a physician could help a terminally ill patient in great discomfort and with no chance of improvement to voluntarily die.

Physician contingency reserve—A monetary set-aside used in health plans in which physicians and other health care providers share financial risk. A certain percentage of funds is withheld from the money paid to a physician for patient care and is paid back to the physician at the end of the year if the physician meets the plan's standards for costs of care and number of patients seen. See also **Withhold.**

Physician executive—A physician who serves on the administrative staff at a health care institution as a liaison between the physicians on staff and the hospital administration.

Physician extender—A health professional, such as a nurse or health educator, who works with patients to make the patient's time with the physician more efficient and productive.

Physician-hospital-community organization (PHCO)—A legal entity formed by at least one local hospital, a group of physicians, and community organizations to reach common goals. Each organization is represented on the board. PHCOs function like PHOs and usually are organized for the purpose of obtaining managed care contracts directly with employers. The PHCO serves as a collective negotiating and contracting unit.

Physician-hospital organization (PHO)—A legal entity sponsored and jointly governed by a hospital and a subset of its medical staff to negotiate and service managed care contracts and achieve administrative efficiencies.

Physician Payment Review Commission (PPRC)—A congressional entity of independent experts created in 1986 to provide advice on Medicare physician payment issues. It established administrative rules, policies, and procedures regarding allowable Medicare charges and was merged into MedPAC in 1997.

Plan physician—A physician who has contracted with or is employed by a health plan to furnish services to members.

Point-of-service (POS) plan—A health care plan that combines the characteristics of indemnity insurance and HMOs. Generally, at the time service is rendered, the insured can elect to receive the service from an HMO network provider at a discount or with no out-of-pocket cost, or from a non-network provider but subject to substantially higher patient cost sharing. See also **Open-ended** or **open-access HMO; Triple-option plan.**

Pooling—The process of combining all claims or cost experience for defined populations or types of coverage (e.g., a school or business) into one risk pool in order to spread the risk or claims liability.

Pool of doctors (POD)—The smaller units or pools into which health plans often group doctors. Many times 10 to 30 physicians may be grouped together as a performance measurement tool.

Population profile—A statistical summary of population-specific health care data used to assess health care delivery.

Portability—An individual's ability to continue health insurance coverage when changing a job or residence without a waiting period or having to meet additional deductible requirements.

Positron emission tomography (PET) scan—An imaging technique that tracks metabolism and responses to therapy used in cardiology, neurology, and oncology.

Practice guidelines—Systematically developed statements on medical practices that assist a practitioner in making decisions about appropriate health care for specific medical conditions. Managed care organizations frequently use these guidelines to evaluate appropriateness and medical necessity of care. Also called *practice parameters.*

Practice pattern—The manner in which an individual provider uses medical resources to treat patients. Increasingly, managed care organizations and hospitals are monitoring physician practice patterns in an attempt to lower utilization of medical services.

Preadmission certification—A process by which a health care professional uses established medical criteria to evaluate an attending physician's request for a patient's admission to a hospital.

Preexisting condition—A physical or mental condition that an insured has prior to the effective date of coverage. Policies may exclude coverage for such conditions for a specified period.

Preferred provider organization (PPO)—A managed care health plan that contracts with networks or panels of providers to furnish services to a defined population and is to be paid on a negotiated fee schedule. Enrollees are offered a financial incentive to use providers on the preferred list but may use non-network providers as well. See also *Managed care.*

Premium—The money a company or person pays to a health plan every month for health insurance. Premiums vary in cost depending on age, sex, health status, number of people in the family, and other factors.

Premium caps—Maximum charges in a reform proposal that limits the amount of money a health plan can charge for a specific set of services. By setting a maximum level that plans can charge for services, the plan will be responsible for managing costs and quality of care and will be competing for consumers on the same basis as other plans.

Prepaid benefit package—The set of health care services that a plan is responsible for providing and for which the plan will receive reimbursement through a per-member-per-month predetermined capitation/premium rate.

Prepaid group practice (PGP) plan—A form of HMO in which specified health services are rendered by participating physicians. Enrollees make fixed periodic payments in advance; or an insurance carrier contracts to pay in advance for the full range of health services to which the enrollee is entitled.

Prepaid health care plan (PHP)—A plan in which a defined set of services is provided for a fixed, periodic payment made in advance of the provision of services. Prepaid health care plans may include HMOs, eye plans, dental plans, and similar plans. Under such plans, the financial risk of delivering the health care is transferred from the purchaser to the health plan.

Prepayment—A method of providing the cost of health care services in advance of their use.

Presents—A term physicians use to describe the symptoms (e.g., headache, fatigue, pain, and so on) a patient has during his or her visit.

Prevalence—The number of cases of a disease or condition existing in a given population at a specific period or moment in time.

Preventive health care—Health care that has as its aim the prevention of disease and illness before it occurs and thus concentrates on keeping patients well.

Primary care—Basic care, including initial diagnosis and treatment, preventive services, maintenance treatment of chronic conditions, and referral to specialists.

Primary care case management (PCCM)—Managed care arrangements in which primary care providers receive a per capita management fee to coordinate a patient's care in addition to reimbursement (fee-for-service or capitation) for the services they provided. PCCM practices may be held at risk for costs of specialists and/or hospital services and are sometimes responsible for treatment authorization and claims payment.

Primary care center—A type of freestanding ambulatory care center that provides primary care on a scheduled basis and is open approximately eight hours a day.

Primary care network (PCN)—A group of primary care physicians (PCPs) who share the risk of providing care to members of a managed care plan. The PCP in a primary care network is accountable for the total health care services of a plan member, including referrals to specialists, supervision of the specialists' care, and hospitalization. Participating PCPs' services are covered by a monthly capitation payment to the PCN.

Primary care physician (PCP)—A general/family practitioner or internist who treats a variety of health problems across all patient age groups and who frequently serves as the patient's first point of contact with the health care system. In some cases, OB/GYNS and pediatricians are considered PCPs, who often serve as gatekeepers under managed care.

Principal diagnosis—An ICDM diagnosis established after study as being chiefly responsible for occasioning the admission of a patient to the hospital for care. Also referred to as the *principal inpatient diagnosis (PID)*.

Prior authorization—A cost-control procedure that requires a service or medication to be approved in advance by the doctor and/or the insurer. Without prior authorization, the health plan or insurer will not pay for the test, drug, or services.

Private inurement—When a not-for-profit business operates in such a way as to provide more than incidental financial gain to a private individual, a practice frowned upon by the IRS.

Private not-for-profit hospital—A not-for-profit hospital owned and operated by a private corporation whose excess of income over expenses is used for hospital purposes rather than returned to shareholders or investors as dividends. Sometimes referred to as a *voluntary hospital.*

Private patient review—An evaluation of the hospital care provided for patients within a specified health plan. The word *private* implies that the health plan is not government-sponsored; that is, Medicare or Medicaid.

Private practice—A traditional arrangement wherein physicians are not employees of any entity and generally treat a variety of patients in terms of their payment sources.

Privileges—Prerogatives of individuals to provide medical or other patient care services in the granting institution, within well-defined limits, based on the individual's professional license, experience, competence, ability, and judgment. Also referred to as *clinical privileges* or *medical staff privileges.*

Productivity—The relationship between service input and output. Typical productivity measures for labor costs include FTEs per patient day, FTEs per admission, and FTEs per bed.

Professional liability insurance (PLI)—Insurance protection for real or alleged errors committed in the practice of a profession (i.e., physician-hospital professional liability).

Professional patient (Munchausen's syndrome)—A person who repeatedly fabricates illness, usually acute, dramatic, and convincing, and goes from hospital to hospital for treatment. A child may be used as a surrogate patient: the parent falsifies a history and may injure the child to simulate an illness or disease or produce a life-threatening emergency.

Profitability—A financial ratio that measures the earning power and earning record of a corporation.

Proprietary hospital—See *For-profit hospital.*

Prospective financing—Financing for health care services based on prices or budgets determined prior to the delivery of service. Payments can be per unit of service, per member, or per period.

Prospective payment—A method of payment for health care services in which the amount of payment for services is set prior to the delivery of those services and the hospital (or other provider) is at least partially at risk for losses or stands to gain from surpluses that accrue in the payment period. Prospective payment rates may be per service, per capita, per diem, or per case rates.

Prospective Payment Assessment Commission (ProPAC)—A group of independent experts appointed by the Congressional Office of Technology to advise Congress on issues relating to the Medicare prospective payment system (PPS), including annual recommendations on the increase in PPS rates. In 1997, ProPAC was merged into the Medicare Payment Advisory Commission (MedPAC), which provides guidance on the program's reimbursement/payment policies generally (e.g., for hospitals, physicians, home health agencies, and so on).

Prospective Payment System (PPS)—Medicare's system, adopted in the Social Security Amendments of 1983, by which hospitals are paid a fixed, prospectively set price for each Medicare beneficiary treated as an inpatient according to the patient's DRG.

Protocols—Standards or practices developed to assist health care providers and patients to make decisions about particular steps in the treatment process.

Provider—A hospital or health care professional who provides health care services to patients. May be an entity (hospital, nursing home, or other facility) or a person, such as a physician or nurse.

Provider-sponsored network (PSN)—Developed by providers, this network may be an IDS consisting of hospitals and physicians or simply physicians. PSNs are formed in an effort to contract directly with employers and government agencies. See also **Provider-sponsored organization (PSO).**

Provider-sponsored organization (PSO)—A health care delivery system owned and operated by providers that integrates a wide spectrum of services and directly contracts with various entities on a managed care basis. See also **Provider-sponsored network (PSN).**

Public Health Service (PHS)—A division of the U.S. Department of Health and Human Services responsible for the health and well-being of the American public by providing services for low-income families and individuals and battling communicable diseases. PHS's responsibility includes environmental health as well as clinical health services to prevent the spread of disease.

Purchaser—An employer or company that buys health insurance for its employees.

Pursue and pay—When a plan does not pay a benefit until alternative sources of payment (e.g., another plan) have been pursued. Also called *chase and pay.*

Qualified employee—An employee who works more than 30 hours per week, or 120 hours per month. Qualified employees usually receive benefits, including health insurance, while temporary, seasonal, or part-time employees do not.

Qualified Medicare beneficiary (QMB)—An individual who qualifies for Medicare and whose income is at or below the poverty level. The state must pay the person's Part B payment as well as copayments and deductibles.

Quality assessment—An activity that monitors the level of health care (including patient, administrative, and support services) provided to plan members and compares it to preestablished criteria for professional performance. The medical record is used as documentation of the care provided.

Quality assurance (QA)—A process designed to objectively and systematically monitor and evaluate the appropriateness of patient care and pursue opportunities to improve patient care and resolve identified problems.

Quality Assurance Reform Initiative (QARI)—An HCFA-sponsored effort to design a more effective approach to monitor and improve the quality of care delivered by managed care plans enrolling Medicaid recipients. QARI includes both a quality assurance framework and clinical guidelines for states.

Quality circle—A small group of employees doing similar work that voluntarily meets regularly to discuss quality problems, analyze the causes, recommend solutions, and, where possible, take action. It is a TQM concept.

Quality improvement program (QIP)—A continuing process of identifying problems in health care delivery and testing and continually monitoring solutions for constant improvement. QIP is a common feature of TQM programs. The aim of QIP is the elimination of variations in health care delivery through the removal of their causes and the elimination of waste through design and redesign processes. See also *Continuous quality improvement (CQI)*.

Quality indicator—A measure of the degree of excellence of the health care actually provided. Selected quality indicators of patient outcome are mortality and morbidity, health status, length of stay, readmission rate, patient satisfaction, and so on.

Quality of care—The degree to which patient care meets accepted principles and standards of practice.

Quality review (QR) committee—A committee established by a professional organization or institution to evaluate and/or ensure the quality of care provided to patients. It can function independently on a broad range of topics related to health care quality.

Rate category—Refers to the specific age/sex cells or cohorts that together make up the total eligible population. Capitation payments to health plans are often made on a rate category-specific basis, particularly for the Medicaid population.

Rate review—Prospective review by a government or private agency of a hospital's budget and financial data, performed for the purpose of determining the reasonableness of the hospital rates and evaluating proposed rate increases.

Rate setting—Determination by a government agency or commission of the rates a hospital may charge private pay patients.

Rationing—The allocation of medical care by price or availability of services.

Reasonable and customary charge—A charge for health care consistent with the prevailing rate or charge in a certain geographical area for identical or similar services. See also *Customary, prevailing, and reasonable (CPR).*

Recidivism—A patient's return to a hospital for the same medical condition or treatment. In substance abuse programs, it describes the patient's return to abusive drug or alcohol use.

Registry—(1) A database on the incidence of specific diseases, patient demographics, treatment protocols, and treatment outcomes for patients with these diagnoses. (2) An official list of individuals with professional standing and/or credentials in specific health care occupations.

Rehabilitation facility—A facility that provides medical, health-related, social, and/or vocational services to disabled persons to help them attain their maximum functional capacity.

Reinstatement—Resumption of coverage under an insurance policy that has lapsed.

Reinsurance—A type of insurance purchased by primary insurers (insurers that provide health care coverage directly to policyholders) from other secondary insurers, called *reinsurers,* to protect against part or all losses the primary insurer might assume in honoring claims of its policyholders. Also known as *excess risk insurance.* See also *Stop-loss insurance.*

Relative value scale (RVS)—An index that assigns weights to each medical service; the weights represent the relative amount to be paid for each service. The RVS used in the Medicare fee schedule consists of three components: physician labor, practice expense, and malpractice expense.

Relative value unit (RVU)—The unit of measure for a relative value scale. RVUs must be multiplied by a dollar conversion factor to establish payment amounts.

Renewal—Continuance of coverage under a policy beyond its original term by the plan's acceptance of the premium for a new policy term.

Report card—An emerging tool that can be used by policymakers and health care purchasers such as employers, government bodies, employer coalitions, and consumers to compare and understand the actual performance of health plans. This tool provides health plan performance data in major areas of accountability such as: quality and utilization, consumer satisfaction, administration efficiency, financial stability, and cost control.

Reserves—The amount of money insurers are required by state or federal law to put aside and hold to ensure their solvency and ability to pay claims.

Resident (medical)—A physician in training who participates in an accredited program of graduate medical education sponsored by a hospital.

Resource-based relative value scale (RBRVS)—A fee schedule for physicians used by Medicare to reflect the value of one service relative to others in terms of the resources required to perform the service.

Respite care—Temporary relief to people who are caring for elderly or disabled relatives who require 24-hour care; that is, offering them a break from their caregiving activities.

Restricted funds—All hospital resources that are restricted to particular purposes by donors and other external authorities. These funds are not available for the financing of general operating activities but may be used in the future when certain conditions and requirements are met. There are three types of restricted funds: specific purpose, plant replacement and expansion, and endowment.

Retention—(1) A health plan's ability to keep its members. (2) The part of a premium that a plan will keep to cover the administrative costs of the program.

Return on assets (ROA)—See *Return on investment.*

Return on equity (ROE)—After-tax earnings of a corporation divided by its shareholders' equity. Shareholders' equity is determined by deducting total liabilities and intangible assets from total assets. ROE is often considered the most important of profitability ratios, and a corporation's objective is to realize a ROE of at least 15 percent in order to provide for dividends and fund future growth.

Return on investment (ROI)—After-tax income for a specified period of time divided by total assets; a financial tool to measure and relate a corporation's earnings to its total asset base.

Risk adjustment—The process used to adjust premium payments to plans to compensate for differences in the health status of enrollees across plans.

Risk analysis—The process of evaluating the predicted costs of medical care for a group under a particular health plan. It aids managed care organizations and insurers in determining which products, benefit levels, and prices to offer in order to best meet the needs of both the group and the plan.

Risk contract—A contract between an HMO/CMP and the HCFA requiring that the health plan provide services to Medicare beneficiaries in return for a fixed monthly payment for enrolled Medicare members. All other services under this contract are provided on an at-risk basis.

Risk corridor—A risk-sharing mechanism by which a provider assumes risk for performance above or below certain established claims targets.

Risk load—A weighting factor used by insurance carriers and managed care plans to calculate premium rates for each enrolled group. The risk load is factored into the premium rate to offset an adverse parameter in the group.

Risk management—An insurance and quality control-related discipline responsible for identification and assessment of loss potential, control and funding, and the management of workers' compensation and claims professionals.

Risk pool—(1) An arrangement by a state to provide health insurance to the unhealthy uninsured who have been rejected for coverage by insurance carriers.

(2) A pool of funds set aside by a managed care plan involved in a risk-sharing arrangement with providers. This pool is created by withholding a portion of provider fees as an incentive to control utilization and to cover any unexpected costs. Funds remaining in the pool after a set period (usually a year) are distributed to the providers.

Risk selection—The process by which health plans differ in the health risk associated with their enrollees because of enrollment choices made by the plans or enrollees. As a result, one health plan's expected costs differ from another's as a result of underlying differences in their enrolled populations.

Risk sharing—A method, such as outlier payments, that places a health plan at less than full risk by covering the cost of selected services, providing additional payment amounts for high-cost patients or to offset plan losses.

Rule of reason—Antitrust test to determine whether the formation of a network is anticompetitive. The network must share substantial financial risk or achieve substantial clinical integration to be considered anticompetitive.

Rural health center—An outpatient facility in a nonurbanized area (per the U.S. Census Bureau) primarily engaged in furnishing physicians' and other medical health services in accordance with certain federal requirements designed to ensure the health and safety of the individuals served by the health center. Rural health centers serve areas designated for their shortage of personal health services or a health workforce.

Rural health network—An organization consisting of at least one critical-access hospital and at least one acute care hospital. Its provider participants enter into agreements regarding patient referral and transfer, the development and use of communication systems, and the provision of emergency and nonemergency transportation.

Rural referral center—Generally large rural hospitals that Medicare designates to serve patients referred by other hospitals or by physicians who are not members of the hospital's medical staff.

Safe harbor regulations—A set of federal regulations that clarify and ease the restrictions of the Medicare/Medicaid antifraud and abuse statute. The regulations specify certain types of provider payment arrangements that are not subject to criminal prosecution or civil sanctions.

Safety zone—The level of physician network concentration under which the Federal Trade Commission (FTC) will not make an antitrust challenge. Physicians in networks falling within the safety zone may negotiate managed care fees collectively.

Sanctions—Negative incentives, such as withholding of funds or exclusion from a practice or hospital. Federal regulation forbids HMOs from using sanctions to reduce costs.

Saturation—A condition that occurs when a health plan achieves its maximum penetration either in a subscriber group or its marketplace.

Seamless care—The experience by patients of smooth and easy movement from one aspect of comprehensive health care to another; care that is notable for the absence of red tape.

Secondary care—Attention given to a person in need of specialty services following referral from a source of primary care.

Secondary coverage—Insurance coverage for an individual who has health care benefits from more than one source, such as from both health insurance and automobile insurance, or from private health insurance and Medicare. After the benefits of the primary coverage are exhausted, the secondary insurer's benefits typically cover the remaining costs.

Secondary diagnosis—An ICD-9-CM-coded condition that exists at the time of admission or develops subsequently that affects the treatment received and/or length of stay.

Second-opinion review—A managed care technique in which a second physician is consulted regarding diagnosis or course of treatment. It is thought to be of questionable effectiveness in reducing costs.

Section 125 plan—Also known as a *flexible benefit plan,* a reference to section 125 of the IRS Code allowing contributions employees make to these plans to be from pretax dollars. Also called *cafeteria benefits.* See also **Flexible benefits.**

Self-Insurance—An insurance method that retains the risk within a hospital or group of hospitals while providing a funding mechanism (similar to a trust fund) to cover the cost of litigation and malpractice liability losses. Another form of self-insurance is nonfunded self-insurance, or "going bare." Under this method, the hospital pays its malpractice losses and related expenses from its operating capital.

Sentinel effect—A scientific phenomenon suggesting that when people know they are being observed, their behavior changes. Utilization is typically reduced when providers realize someone is watching.

Sentinel event—An unexpected occurrence or variation involving death or serious physical or psychological injury, or such a risk to a patient. Serious injury includes loss of limb or function. The event is called "sentinel" because it sounds a warning that requires immediate attention. The JCAHO is requesting the voluntary reporting of such events by accredited health care organizations.

Service area—The geographic area a health plan serves. Some insurers are statewide or national, while others operate in specific counties or communities.

Service bureau—A form of integrated delivery system in which a hospital (or other organization) provides services to a physician's practice in return for a fair market price. May be used to negotiate with managed care plans but is not considered an effective negotiating mechanism.

Service contracts—Agreements wherein hospitals contract with individual physicians or groups of physicians to provide certain services.

Service plans—Health plans (typically the Blues) that have direct contracts with providers but are not necessarily managed care plans. The service contracts mean the provider bills the plan and is paid only the plan's usual and customary fees.

Shadow pricing—An unethical and sometimes illegal practice of setting premium fees at a level near or below a competitor's rate without having the rates developed or justified by an actuary.

Shared services—Administrative, clinical, or service functions that are common to two or more health care institutions and used jointly or cooperatively by them in some manner for the purpose of improving service, containing cost, and/or effecting economies of scale.

Single payer—One entity (usually the government) that functions as the only purchaser of health care services.

Single-specialty group—A group consisting only of physicians practicing the same specialty.

Site-of-service differential—The difference in the amount paid to the physician when the same service is performed in different practice settings (e.g., a colonoscopy in a physician's office or a hospital clinic).

Skilled nursing facility (SNF)—A facility that provides acute 24-hour medical care and continuous nursing care services and various other health and social services to patients who are not in the acute phase of illness and require primarily convalescent, rehabilitative, and/or restorative services. The care may be delivered in a freestanding facility or in a unit of a hospital.

Skimming—The act of encouraging the enrollment of healthy, "low-risk" individuals in prepaid health plans while discouraging the enrollment of sick individuals, often accomplished through risk selection. See also *Cherry picking.*

Social health maintenance organization (SHMO)—An HCFA demonstration project that expands the Medicare benefit package to reduce or slow functional impairment of frail beneficiaries. Additional covered services include nursing home, homemaker, transportation, drugs, and case management services.

Social insurance—An insurance system in which funds are pooled and transferred to a government organization that provides benefits and administers the program for all citizens.

Socialized medicine—A system of medical care regulated and controlled by the government for the entire population at no, or low, direct cost to individuals as a result of tax subsidies.

Sole community provider (SCP)—A hospital that is the sole source of inpatient care reasonably available to Part A Medicare beneficiaries in a geographic area as a result of its isolation, absence of other facilities, and weather or travel conditions. Also referred to as a *sole community hospital (SCH)*.

Solo practice—A medical practice in which sole responsibility for practice decisions and management falls to the independent physician.

Specialist—A physician whose training focuses on a particular area rather than family medicine or general medicine. Specialists work at the secondary level of health care and provide services not all physicians can perform. Specialties include urology, dermatology, and cardiology.

Special needs plan (SNP)—A managed care network established specifically to serve defined populations, such as HIV+, individuals who are seriously and persistently mentally ill (SPMI), or seriously emotionally disturbed (SED). States may contract with SNP managed care networks under the authority of a Section 1115(a) waiver on approval by the HCFA.

Specialty medical group (SMG)—A single-specialty group of physicians or a multi-specialty group of physicians.

Specialty network—A managed care network in which certain types of services, such as organ transplants, spinal and head injury care, specialized orthopedic surgery (e.g., total hip replacement), and chemical dependency treatment programs, are separated out from a managed care plan for procedure- or service-specific contracting. Specialty network providers are selected based on criteria and standards set by the payers.

Specific-purpose fund—A type of restricted fund that includes all resources restricted by donors to the financing of charity service, educational programs, research projects, and other specific purposes other than endowments and plant asset acquisition.

Spend-down—The intentional depletion of income or assets by people so they can become eligible for Medicaid coverage, particularly to support nursing home care.

Sponsorship—A relationship between a religious or other sponsoring organization and a hospital that may set limits on the activities undertaken within the hospital or is intended to further the objectives of the sponsoring organization but does not involve ownership or other legal relationships.

Staffing ratio—The total number of hospital FTEs divided by the average daily census.

Staff model HMO—A model in which physicians are employed directly by the HMO and provide services in HMO-owned or -managed clinics. These physicians typically serve HMO members exclusively and receive a salary plus a bonus based on the HMO's performance and/or profits. See also ***Capitation; Group model HMO; Health maintenance organization (HMO); Independent practice association (IPA) model HMO.***

Standard Industry Code (SIC)—A categorization of businesses by industry type that helps in setting health insurance rates based on associated levels of risk.

Standard of care—In a medical malpractice action, the degree of reasonable skill, care, and diligence exercised by members of the same health profession practicing in the same or similar locality in light of the present state of medical or surgical science.

State mandates—See *Mandated benefits.*

State plan—The comprehensive written statement submitted to HCFA by each state Medicaid agency describing the nature and scope of its Medicaid program. Also referred to as the *state Medicaid plan.*

Step-down unit—A specialized intensive nursing unit that accommodates the same monitoring and patient support equipment as an intensive care unit but with a higher ratio of patients to nurses. Its use is determined by establishing threshold values for the volume of care required. See also *Intensive care unit (ICU).*

Stop-loss insurance—An insurance policy designed to reimburse a self-funded arrangement of one or more small employers for catastrophic, excess, or unexpected expenses. Neither the employees nor other individuals are third-party beneficiaries under the policy. Also known as *excess risk insurance.* See also *Reinsurance.*

Strategic planning—A long-range, comprehensive, and structured decision process that ensures logical steps within a time frame for reaching desired goals by the weighing of each decision step against alternative choices.

Subacute care—Medical and skilled nursing services provided to patients who are not in an acute phase of illness but require a level of care higher than that provided in a long-term care setting.

Subcapitation—A payment method that allows network HMOs to shift more risk of excessive care costs to the doctors and specialists who would gain financially if the care for a patient's illness does not exceed the capitated fixed payment budget. This method may create an incentive for these providers to withhold necessary care.

Subrogation—A process that allows primary insurers to collect funds from secondary or tertiary insurers for health care expenses.

Subscriber—The individual who is responsible for payment of premiums or whose employment is the basis for eligibility for membership in a group health plan. The term *subscriber* does not refer to covered dependents who are members. See also *Member.*

Substantial portion—As defined by the HCFA, at least 70 percent of the required benefits under Part A and Part B of Medicare and the portion that a provider-sponsored organization must directly provide.

Super PHO—A structure in which individual local physician-hospital organizations join together to form one large regional PHO.

Support services—Services other than medical, nursing, and ancillary services that provide support in the delivery of clinical services for patient care (e.g., housekeeping, food service, and security).

Surcharge—An additional charge for optional or supplemental services provided over and above previously agreed upon charges for specified services.

Surgicenter—See *Freestanding ambulatory surgery center.*

Swing beds—Acute care hospital beds that can also be used for long-term care, depending on the needs of the patient and the community. Only those hospitals with fewer than 100 beds and located in a rural community, where long-term care may be inaccessible, are eligible to have swing beds under Medicare. See also *Bed conversion.*

Swipe cards—Cards such as those used in banking for cash machines or automated teller machines. Health care swipe cards, if adopted, would be coded with a person's health plan, benefit levels, cost-sharing requirements, and other health-related information.

Tax Equity and Fiscal Responsibility Act of 1982 (TEFRA)—The federal law that limits the amount of all hospital inpatient costs per discharge under Medicare and mandated the development of a prospective pricing system for hospitals. It also created the current risk and cost provisions in HCFA's contracts with health plans. TEFRA extended Medicare payment limits to ancillary services, added Medicare coverage of hospice care, and allowed Medicare to sign risk contracts with HMOs and competitive medical plans.

Teaching hospital—A hospital that has an accredited physician residency training program, typically affiliated with a medical school.

Telemedicine—An emerging technology that allows medical services to be conducted over a great geographic distance (e.g., rural areas that often lack specialists) by using electronic or other media to transmit images or information.

Tertiary care—Medical care of a highly technological and specialized nature provided in a medical center or teaching and research institution for patients with severe, complicated, or unusual medical problems.

Therapeutic equivalents—Medications that have the same effect on a patient even though the drug products may be different.

Third-party administrator (TPA)—The administration of a group insurance plan by some person or firm other than the insurer or policyholder.

Third-party payer—An organization that acts as a fiscal intermediary between the provider and consumer of care. Examples include insurance carriers, HMOs, and government as a provider of Medicare and Medicaid.

Total capitation—See *Global capitation.*

Total quality management (TQM)—A long-term corporate strategy focusing on the continuous improvement of key work processes that ultimately improve products and services, foster efficiency and team involvement, and satisfy the needs and expectations of customers.

Traditional indemnity insurance—The traditional type of health insurance in which the insured is reimbursed for covered expenses without regard to choice of provider.

Transfer provision—A provision in the Balanced Budget Act of 1997 that reduced Medicare hospital payment under 10 leading DRGs from full PPS rates to per diem rates for early patient transfers (i.e., discharges made prior to the standard length of stay from an inpatient facility to a rehabilitation facility or skilled nursing facility or for home health visits within three days after discharge). HCFA also attempted to include swing beds in the transfer category but was rebuffed by Congress.

Trauma center—A facility providing emergency and specialized intensive care to critically ill and injured patients.

Triage—The sorting and allocation of treatment to patients, especially disaster victims, according to a system of priorities designed to maximize the number of survivors.

Triple option plan—A type of managed care plan that allows members to choose any of three service options—HMO, PPO, or indemnity plan—each time they require medical care. A primary care physician manages accountability for care. An advantage of a triple option plan for employers is that it features a single set of benefits administered through a single carrier. See also *Point-of-service (POS) plan.*

Trustee—A member of a hospital governing body. May also be referred to as a *director* or *commissioner.*

Turnaround time (TAT)—The amount of time it takes a health plan to process and pay a claim from the time it arrives.

Unbundling—A prohibited practice used by some providers to charge more for a service by billing separately for each of its component procedures.

Uncompensated care—Care for which the provider is not compensated. Generally, uncompensated care includes charity care and bad debts (uncollectible charges to patients who have the ability to pay). See also *Indigent care; Medically indigent.*

Underinsured—A descriptive term for people who may have some type of health care insurance, such as catastrophic care, but lack coverage for ordinary health care costs.

Underwriting—The process of identifying, evaluating, and classifying the potential level of risk represented by a person or group seeking insurance coverage in order to determine appropriate pricing, the risk involved, and administrative feasibility.

Uniform benefit plans—Health plans that offer the same basic package of preventive and acute care benefits. Plan enrollees may pay additional premiums for coverage of additional services.

Uniform billing (UB-92) code—A code that outlines the specific billing procedure hospitals must follow and list on each patient invoice.

Uniform clinical data set (UCDS)—An HCFA initiative that involves the collection of approximately 1,800 data elements describing patient demographic characteristics, clinical history, clinical findings, and therapeutic intervention. The data are obtained from the medical records of Medicare beneficiaries.

Uninsurable—Description of persons an insurance company does not want to insure, usually because of bad health.

Uninsured—Individuals who do not have health insurance coverage of any type. Over 80 percent of the uninsured are working adults and their family members, of which over 25 percent are children under 18. The uninsured usually earn too much to qualify for public assistance but too little to afford coverage.

Universal access/coverage—The provision of a standard minimum level of health care benefits to all individuals residing in a region, state, or the United States as a whole.

Unrestricted fund—All hospital resources that are not restricted to particular purposes by donors or other external authorities and are available for the financing of general operating activities.

Upcoding—The process of making a false diagnosis of a patient that is in the best interest of the provider in terms of higher reimbursement.

Upper limit/upper-payment limit—Under Medicaid managed care contracts, the amount it would have cost to provide the same services under fee-for-service Medicaid to an actuarially equivalent population. Medicaid payments to managed care plans cannot exceed the upper-payment limit for eligible enrollees.

Urgent care center—A freestanding emergency care facility that may be sponsored by a hospital, a physician(s), or a corporate entity. Sometimes referred to as a *minor emergency facility* or *urgicenter.*

Usual, customary, and reasonable (UCR)—Criteria used by private insurers primarily under fee-for-service arrangements to pay physicians based on charges commonly used by physicians in a local community. Sometimes called *customary, prevailing, and reasonable charges.*

Utilization—Patterns of use for a particular medical service such as hospital care or physician visits.

Utilization management (UM)—The systematic process used by managed care plans to review and regulate patients' use of medical services and providers' use of medical resources. UM includes a variety of techniques, such as second surgical opinion, preadmission certification, concurrent review, case management, discharge planning, and retrospective chart review.

Utilization rate—The volume of health care services used within a specific time period by a given population, usually expressed as the number of units of service used per year per 1,000 persons eligible for the services.

Utilization review (UR)—An evaluation of the care and services that patients receive based on preestablished criteria and standards.

Utilization Review Accreditation Commission (URAC)—A national organization that reviews and accredits utilization review agencies.

Utilization review organization (URO)—An organization that conducts utilization review (UR) activities for managed care organizations. UROs determine certification of an admission, extension of stay in a medical facility, or provision of other health care services for a plan member.

Variable cost—Any cost that varies with output or organizational activity (e.g., labor and materials).

Vertical integration—The combination of different types of providers to make available a comprehensive array of services. Full vertical integration exists when the full continuum of care is represented.

Veterans Affairs, Department of (VA)—An independent division of the federal government that offers health care services to military personnel who have been injured in action or while on active service. It is separate from the Department of Defense and includes hospitals as well as outpatient care and nursing home care. Formerly known as the *Veterans Administration.*

Volunteer (in-service)—A person who serves a hospital without financial remuneration and who, under the direction of the volunteer services department or committee, augments but does not replace paid personnel and professional staff.

Waiver—(1) A provision in a health insurance policy in which specific medical conditions a person already has are excluded from coverage. (2) A process by which states may receive permission from the federal government to provide services not otherwise covered by Medicaid or in a manner different from the rules established by the Social Security Act. Some managed care programs require waivers if, for example, they are mandatory programs or if the state wants to create a period of guaranteed coverage.

Wellness program—A program that encourages health promotion.

Wholistic health—See *Holistic health.*

Withhold—The at-risk portion of a claim that is deducted and withheld by the managed care plan before payment is made to a participating physician for medical services provided to a plan member. The withhold is intended to serve as an incentive for appropriate utilization and quality of care. The amount (usually 20 percent of the claim) remains within the plan and is credited to the doctor's account and awarded at year-end based on a determination that the physician has met plan standards. See also *Physician contingency reserve.*

Working capital—A company's amount of capital available for spending. Detailed as part of the statement of cash flows and the balance sheet, it is current assets less current liabilities.

Wraparound benefits—The portion of a benefits package that is not included in the health plan's capitation but instead is funded on a fee-for-service basis.

Wraparound plan—Insurance or health plan coverage for copays or deductibles that are not covered under a member's base plan. Often used for Medicare.

Year 2000 computer problem (Y2K bug)—A computer hardware glitch that fails to distinguish the year 2000 from the year 1900 because it reads only the last two digits and has been encoded to capture it as a twentieth century (1900–1999) piece of information. Computerized devices that may produce inaccurate results and malfunction as a result of this problem include computers themselves, biomedical and diagnostic equipment, elevators, and robots. Organizations are working to remedy the problem before the year 2000.

HEALTH CARE ABBREVIATIONS AND ACRONYMS

AAFP—American Academy of Family Physicians

AAHP—American Association of Health Plans

AAHSA—American Association of Homes and Services for the Aging

AAMC—Association of American Medical Colleges

AAPCC—adjusted average per capita cost

AAPI—American Accreditation Program, Inc.

AAPPO—American Association of Preferred Provider Organizations

AARP—American Association of Retired Persons

ABA—American Bar Association

ABIM—American Board of Internal Medicine

ACCME—Accreditation Council on Continuing Medical Education

ACG—ambulatory care group

ACGME—Accreditation Council for Graduate Medical Education

ACHE—American College of Healthcare Executives

ACR—adjusted community rating

ACU—ambulatory care unit

ADAMHA—Alcohol, Drug Abuse and Mental Health Administration (DHHS)

ADC—average daily census

ADHC—adult day health care

ADL—activities of daily living

ADR—adverse drug reaction

ADS—alternative delivery system

AFDC—Aid to Families with Dependent Children

AFL-CIO—American Federation of Labor–Committee for Industrial Organizations

AGPA—American Group Practice Association

AHA—American Hospital Association

AHC—academic health center

AHCA—American Health Care Association

AHCPR—Agency for Health Care Policy and Research (DHHS)

AHSR—Association for Health Services Research

AIA—American Institute of Architects

AICPA—American Institute of Certified Public Accountants

AIDS—acquired immune deficiency syndrome

ALOS—average length of stay

AMA—against medical advice

AMA—American Medical Association

AMCP—Association of Managed Care Providers

AMHO—Association of Managed Health Care Organizations

AMI—American Medical International

ANA—American Nurses Association

AOA—American Osteopathic Association

AOHA—American Osteopathic Hospital Association

AONE—American Organization of Nurse Executives

A/P—accounts payable

APC—ambulatory patient classifications

APD—adjusted patient day

APG—ambulatory patient group

A/R—accounts receivable

ARC—AIDS-related complex

ASAE—American Society of Association Executives

ASC—ambulatory surgical center

ASO—Administrative services only (contract)

BBA—Balanced Budget Act of 1997

BC/BS—Blue Cross and Blue Shield

BLS—Bureau of Labor Statistics

BME—Board of Medical Examiners

BMQA—Board of Medical Quality Assurance

CAE—certified association executive

CAH—critical access hospital

CAP—College of American Pathologists

CAT (CT)—computerized axial tomography (scan)

CBO—Congressional Budget Office

CCN—Community Care Network℠*

CCU—critical care unit

CDC—Centers for Disease Control and Prevention

CE—continuing education

CEO—chief executive officer

CFO—chief financial officer

CHA—Catholic Health Association of the United States

CHAMPUS—Civilian Health and Medical Program of the Uniformed Services

CHAP—Child Health Assurance Program

CHF—congestive heart failure

CHIN—Community Health Information Network

CHIP—Children's Health Insurance Program

CICU—coronary intensive care unit

CIO—chief information officer

CLIA—Clinical Laboratory Improvement Amendment of 1988

CM—case management; case manager

CME—continuing medical education

CMP—competitive medical plan

CNM—certified nurse midwife

CNS—clinical nurse specialist

COA—certificate of authority

COB—coordination of benefits

---

*Community Care Network, Inc., uses the name Community Care Network℠ as its service mark and reserves all rights.

COBRA—Consolidated Omnibus Budget Reconciliation Act of 1985

COE—center of excellence

COLA—cost-of-living adjustment

CON—certificate of need

COO—chief operating officer

CORF—comprehensive outpatient rehabilitation facility

COTH—Council of Teaching Hospitals

CPA—certified public accountant

CPHA—Commission on Professional and Hospital Activities

CPHO—community physician-hospital organization

CPI—consumer price index

CPR—cardiopulmonary resuscitation

CPR—customary, prevailing, and reasonable (fees)

CPT—Current Procedural Terminology

CQI—continuous quality improvement

CRNA—chief registered nurse anesthetist

CT—computerized tomography

CVO—credentialing verification organization

CY—calendar year

D&O—directors' and officers' (liability coverage)

DEA—Drug Enforcement Administration

DHHS—Department of Health and Human Services

DME—director of medical education

DME—durable medical equipment

DNR—do not resuscitate

DO—doctor of osteopathy

DOA—dead on arrival

DOD—Department of Defense

DOJ—Department of Justice

DOL—Department of Labor

DOT—Department of Transportation

DPR—drug price review

DRG—diagnosis-related group

DSH—disproportionate share adjustment

DUR—drug utilization review

Dx—diagnosis

ECF—extended care facility

ECU—environmental control unit

ED—emergency department

EDP—electronic data processing

EDS—electronic data system

EEG—electroencephalogram

EEOC—Equal Employment Opportunity Commission

EKG—electrocardiogram

EMG—electromyogram

EMS—emergency medical system (or services)

EMT—emergency medical technologist

EMTALA—Emergency Medical Treatment and Active Labor Act

EOB—explanation of benefits

EOC—evidence of coverage

EPA—Environmental Protection Agency

EPO—exclusive provider organization

EPSDT—Early and Periodic Screening, Diagnosis and Treatment (program)

ER—emergency room

ERISA—Employee Retirement Income Security Act of 1974

ESRD—end-stage renal disease

FACCT—Foundation for Accountability

FACHE—fellow of the American College of Healthcare Executives

FAHS—Federation of American Health Systems

FAR—federal acquisition regulations

FASB—Financial Accounting Standards Board

FDA—Food and Drug Administration

FEC—freestanding emergency center

FFS—fee-for-service reimbursement

FI—fiscal intermediary

FMG—foreign medical graduate

FP—family practitioner; family practice

FQHC—federally qualified health center

FQHMO—federally qualified health maintenance organization

FTC—Federal Trade Commission

FTE—full-time equivalent (personnel)

FY—fiscal year

FYE—fiscal year end(ing)

GAAP—generally accepted accounting principles

GAO—General Accounting Office

GDP—gross domestic product

GI—gastrointestinal

GME—graduate medical education

GNC—general nursing care

GNP—gross national product

GPWW—group practice without walls

GSA—group service agreement

HCFA—Health Care Financing Administration (DHHS)

HCPCS—HCFA Common Procedural Coding System

HCSP—health care service plan

HCW—health care worker

HEDIS—Health Plan Employer Data and Information Set

HFMA—Healthcare Financial Management Association

HHS—Health and Human Services Department

HHS—home health services

HI—hospital (or health) insurance

HIAA—Health Insurance Association of America

HIO—health-insuring organization

HIP—health insurance plan

HIPAA—Health Insurance Portability and Accountability Act of 1996

HIPC—health insurance purchasing cooperative

HMBI—hospital market basket index

HMO—health maintenance organization

HPA—hospital-physician alliance

HPDP—health promotion and disease prevention

HPEAA—Health Professions Educational Assistance Act

HRET—Health Research and Educational Trust

IBNR—incurred but not reported

ICCU—intensive coronary care unit

ICD-9-CM—International Classification of Diseases, 9th Revision, Clinical Modification

ICD-10-CM—International Classification of Diseases, 10th Revision, Clinical Modification

ICF—intermediate care facility

ICN—intermediate care nursery

ICU—intensive care unit

IDS—integrated delivery system

IG—Inspector General

IHO—integrated health care organization

IME—indirect medical education

IMG—international medical graduate

IOM—Institute of Medicine

I/P—inpatient

IP—integrated provider

IPA—independent practice association

IRA—individual retirement account

IRS—Internal Revenue Service

IS—information system

IV—intravenous

JCAHO—Joint Commission on Accreditation of Healthcare Organizations

JCC—joint conference committee

LOA—leave of absence

LOH—length of hospitalization

LOS—length of stay

LPN—licensed practical nurse

LTC—long-term care

LVN—licensed vocational nurse

MAC—maximum allowable cost

MAP—medical audit program

MBO—management by objectives

MCO—managed care organization

MCP—managed care plan

MD—doctor of (allopathic) medicine

MEC—medical executive committee

MedPAC—Medicare Payment Advisory Commission

MEPS—Medical Expenditure Panel Study

MeSH—medical staff-hospital organization

MET—multiple employer trust

MEWA—multiple employer welfare association

MGCRB—Medicare Geographic Classification Review Board

MHA—master of healthcare administration (degree)

MHCA—Managed Health Care Association

MI—myocardial infarction

MIA—medically indigent adult

MICU—mobile intensive care unit

MIP—managed indemnity plan

MIS—management information system

MMIS—Medicaid Management Information System

MLP—midlevel practitioner

MOB—medical office building

MOS—medical outcomes study

MPCC—Medicare per capita cost

MPH—master of public health (degree)

MRA—medical records administration

MRI—magnetic resonance imaging

MRT—medical records technician

MSA—medical savings account

MSA—metropolitan statistical area

MSG—multispecialty group

MSO—management service organization

NA—nursing assistant

NAHDO—National Association of Health Data Organizations

NAHMOR—National Association of HMO Regulators

NAIC—National Association of Insurance Commissioners

NAS—National Academy of Sciences

NB—newborn

NBME—National Board of Medical Examiners

NCHS—National Center for Health Statistics (DHHS)

NCHSR—National Center for Health Services Research (DHHS)

NCQA—National Committee for Quality Assurance

NDC—National Drug Code

NE—nurse executive

NHC—National Health Council

NHSC—National Health Service Corps

NICU—neonatal intensive care unit

NIH—National Institutes of Health (DHHS)

NLN—National League for Nursing

NLRB—National Labor Relations Board

NMHPA—Newborns' and Mothers' Health Protection Act of 1996

NMR—nuclear magnetic resonance

NP—nurse practitioner

NPDB—National Practitioner Data Bank

NTBR—not to be resuscitated

OB/GYN—obstetrics and gynecology

OBRA—Omnibus Budget Reconciliation Act

OD—doctor of optometry

OEO Office of Economic Opportunity

OIG—Office of Inspector General (DHHS)

OMB—Office of Management and Budget

OMC—Office of Managed Care (HCFA)

OMS—outcomes management systems

OOP—out-of-pocket payments

OP—outpatient

OPD—outpatient department

OR—operating room

ORHP—Office of Rural Health Policy (DHHS)

ORT—Operation Restore Trust (DOJ/DHHS)

OSA—optional segregated account

OSHA—Occupational Safety and Health Administration

OT—occupational therapy

OTC—over-the-counter (drugs)

PA—physician's assistant

PAC—political action committee

P&L—profit and loss

PAS—Professional Activity Study

PAT—preadmission testing

PBM—pharmacy benefit management

PC—personal computer

PCCM—primary care case management

PCN—primary care network

PCP—primary care physician/ practitioner/provider

PDR—physicians' desk reference

PET—positron emission tomography (scan)

PGP—prepaid group practice

PGY—postgraduate year

PHCO—physician-hospital-community organization

PHO—physician-hospital organization

PHP—prepaid health care plan

PHS—Public Health Service (DHHS)

PIP—periodic interim payment

PIP—principal inpatient diagnosis

PMPM—per member per month

PMPY—per member per year

POD—pool of doctors

POS—point of service

PPA—preferred provider arrangement

PPM—physician practice management company

PPO—preferred provider organization

PPRC—Physician Payment Review Commission

PPS—prospective payment system

PRHB—postretirement health benefit

PRN—as (often as) or if necessary

PRO—peer review organization

ProPAC—Prospective Payment Assessment Commission

PRRB—Provider Reimbursement Review Board

PSN—provider-sponsored network

PSO—provider-sponsored organization

PSRO—Professional Standards Review Organization

PT—physical therapy

QA—quality assurance

QAP—quality assurance professional

QARI—Quality Assurance Reform Initiative

QC—quality control

QI—quality improvement

QIP—quality improvement program

QMB—qualified Medicare beneficiary

QR—quality review

RAD—radiation absorbed dose

R&D—research and development

RBRVS—resource-based relative value scale

RFP—request for proposal

RHC—rural health clinic

RIF—reduction in force

RN—registered nurse

ROA—return on assets

ROI—return on investment

RPh—registered pharmacist

RPT—registered physical therapist

RRA—registered records administrator

RRT—registered respiratory therapist

RT—respiratory therapist/therapy

RVS—relative value scale

RVU—relative value unit

Rx—prescription

S&P—Standard and Poor's

SCP—sole community provider

SEC—Securities and Exchange Commission

SEIU—Service Employees International Union

SHCC—State Health Coordinating Council

SHMO—social health maintenance organization

SICU—surgical intensive care unit

SIDS—sudden infant death syndrome

SMG—specialty medical group

SMI—supplementary medical insurance

SNF—skilled nursing facility

SNP—special needs plan

SPECT—single photon emission computed tomography

SSA—Social Security Administration

SSDI—Social Security disability insurance

SSI—supplemental security income

STD—sexually transmitted disease

T&E—travel and expense

TAT—turnaround time

TEFRA—Tax Equity and Fiscal Responsibility Act of 1982

TPA—third-party administrator

TQI—total quality improvement

TQM—total quality management

UAP—unlicensed assistive personnel

UB—uniform billing

UBI—unrelated business income

UBIT—unrelated business income tax

UBPS—uniform bill patient summary

UCDS—uniform clinical data set

UCR—usual, customary, and reasonable (charges)

UM—utilization management

UR—utilization review

URAC—Utilization Review Accreditation Commission

URO—utilization review organization

VA—Department of Veterans Affairs

VHA—Voluntary Hospitals of America

VNA—visiting nurses association

VPS—volume performance standard

WC—workers' compensation

WHO—World Health Organization

YTD—year-to-date

Y2K—year 2000 computer bug problem

ZEBRA—zero-balanced reimbursement account